Praise for *Cool Time*

"I am 139 pages into your bo   shape
what I've been trying to impro   ly the
organization of my day. My inb   ......ply all week because I
am organizing my tasks into workable time slots. My clients' regular
call-backs are much quicker and there has been a direct increase in
prospective business for August because I've scheduled in keystone
prospecting time into my day between 1 and 2pm.... your ideas are
making an immediate impact on my daily life, thank you!"

— Ian Turgeon, Hotel Sales Manager, Fairmont Royal York, Toronto

"I took *Cool Time* home last weekend, and have instituted its principles over the last week, and I LOVE IT! I would love to have Steve
Prentice on the show. Is he touring? I have roughly two dozen time
management books, and I hate them all. His is the only one I've ever
truly liked and believed in. It's a godsend, and I MUST share it with
my viewers."

— Bridget Weiss, TV Producer, Edmonton

"I very much enjoyed your session and found a number of different
things that I feel I can utilize to help me get more efficient and effective as both a worker and manager.

The process of blocking time in my calendar for keystone work
as well as the follow-up things (phone, email) really works well for
me and for the environment in which I work... I love the 55-minute
meeting concept and actually spoke to a direct report of mine and
asked her to utilize the concepts in a meeting we have coming up next
week."

— Marina Papadimitrios, Manager, Supply Management, AstraZeneca

"I met Steve the weekend of the 'Great Blackout of 2003.' At that time, all of us across North America were still shaking our heads, wondering how we could have been caught without lights or power and with practically no back-up plan.

Steve appeared on my radio show and quickly taught us the *Cool Time* principles. He was immediately flooded with calls. Listeners wanted to talk to him because he brought such practical advice, common sense and a level head about him. Everything he said made sense! It was an enlightening hour that I've never forgotten. Steve is now a regular guest on my show.

Steve's approach to crisis and everyday living is truly inspiring, rewarding and exciting. Spending time with Steve and his *Cool Time* concept is like getting permission to stop the stress."
— *Christina Cherneskey, Talk Show Host, News Talk 1010 CFRB, Toronto*

"I have been applying the Cool Time principles for a month or so now and have managed to 'find' more time in my days for constructive pursuits and less stress during the evenings. I have recommended your book to my colleagues and associates whenever the challenges of work-life balance or stress management arise."
— *Walter Robinson, Past Federal Director, Canadian Taxpayers Federation*

COOL TIME

A Hands-on Plan for Managing Work and Balancing Time

STEVE PRENTICE

John Wiley & Sons Canada, Ltd.

Copyright © 2005 by Steve Prentice

Library and Archives Canada Cataloguing in Publication Data

Prentice, Steven
Cool Time: a hands-on plan for managing work and balancing time / Steve Prentice.

Includes index
ISBN-13 978-0-470-83673-6
ISBN-10 0-470-83673-3

1. Time management. I. Title.
HD69.T54P739 2005   650.1'1   C2005-902784-3

Production Credits:
Cover design and interior text design: Mike Chan

Printer: Printcrafters Inc.

John Wiley & Sons Canada, Ltd.
6045 Freemont Blvd.
Mississauga, Ontario
L5R 4J3

Printed in Canada

10 9 8 7 6 5 4 3 2

f o $\mathcal{R}$: $\mathcal{M}y$ $f$amily

$\mathcal{T}$ H A N K S T O: Allison Block, Vanni Bronca, Arnold Gosewich, Nelson Hudes, Dr. Jack Muskat, Carol Oblak, France Raymond and Roz Usheroff

QUICK REFERENCE

CONTENTS

A NOTE ABOUT GENDER: For ease of reading, when referring to people, the text alternates between female and male gender, rather than use "his/her" and other awkward combinations. Obviously, the examples and techniques in this book apply to everyone, and no slight or bias is intended.

COOL-TIME.COM: The cool-time website is your ongoing source of Time Management tips, ideas, and resources. As a reader of *Cool Time* I hope you will take time to visit and to contribute your thoughts and ideas.

The website address is: www.cool-time.com

Your username and ID is:
User Name: reader
Password: cooltime

INTRODUCTION

Cool Time refers to the art and science of never breaking a sweat, either mentally or physically, as you go about your day. Cool Time is the end result of the state of mind and attitude brought about by the techniques in this book. It's your investment in excellence.

Working, traveling, and speaking in Cool Time ensures that the highest, most useful faculties of your mind are present and ready. Stress, anger, confusion, and frustration can be controlled by proper planning, anticipation of contingencies, time lines, and constraints, and acknowledging where you are and where you're supposed to be.

Why is this so important? Quite simply, it's an edge. Most people just "get by." You see them running for buses or getting angrier and angrier while stuck in traffic. You see them eating their lunches at their desks. You see them buying headache and stomach remedies to counteract what stress is doing to their bodies. You see them counting down the days until Friday, when they can finally get some rest. These people—your colleagues, clients, and competitors—have the relationship reversed so that stress, anger, confusion, and frustration are front and center on their personal playing field, with clear thought and optimum potential on the sidelines. You will encounter hundreds of examples daily in which people are just hanging on, no longer in control of their own lives. This is no way to exist, and it's certainly no way to get ahead. Stress pushes away the ladder of success, leaving the key components undisturbed on the top shelf.

You, however, now have the power to change that by living in Cool Time.

As a person working and living in Cool Time, you'll still have to deal with crises, managers, deadlines, and delays. But it is the manner in which you handle them that will be different. Your calm, competent air will be looked up to, will be interpreted by some as charisma or leadership quality, which some people seem to have and others lack. Your mannerisms and mindset, now able to ride the chaos and confusion of the day, will make themselves obvious to others, with a brighter sparkle in your eyes, with body language and posture that displays confidence and ability, with a voice that conveys credibility and authority, and with decisions, ideas, and actions that demonstrate excellence.

CHAPTER 1
QUICK! LOOK OVER THERE!

Try saying these words, with some urgency, to a dog. Then point to the horizon. The odds are he'll look at the end of your finger in the hopes that there's food on it. Or he might jump around excitedly, knowing he is supposed to be looking somewhere, but not sure as to which direction that might be. He would certainly not think to follow the direction of your pointing finger, and could not begin to understand that there might be a reward for looking in that direction. For him, his sole interest in the pointing finger is the possibility that you might give him food. Once he sees that there is none, the finger holds no more attraction.

The solutions offered by traditional time management courses and books are very much like that: There's a message there, and some real solutions, but they point to distant concepts and ignore immediate motivations. They place too much emphasis on agendas, prioritization, activity logs, and filing systems, and although these things do have a place in the overall plan, they are just tools, to be employed later, after we have dealt with the primary time management problem—people.

No agenda system, day planner, or mantra of any kind will work if the *people* who assign you the tasks and add to the pressure aren't central to the solution. It's like trying to organize a collection of feathers on a windy day. There's no point in organizing and prioritizing things if we can't do something about outside influences.

CHAPTER 1

To add to that, time is not what it used to be. The information age has changed the traditional approaches to work, health, and life, and has replaced it with a confusing mix of priorities, pressures, and insecurities. People feel compelled to check their e-mail even when they're on vacation. Their cars become mobile offices. If they eat at work, they eat over the keyboard. And by 10:30 a.m. another carefully planned day degenerates into chaos.

All of this happens even though there are more methods, products, and tools to manage one's calendar than ever before.

The reason is very basic and very ancient. As human beings, our body type hasn't changed much in terms of design in the last 50,000 years. Our mind, nervous system, and stomach still react as they did when making fire was big news. Though our collective knowledge has progressed enough to invent computers and nuclear power, our inner workings have not kept pace. We jump every time an e-mail arrives because it's a new stimulus, just like a noise in the bushes. Similarly, in many parts of the world, we are collectively gaining too much weight because our innate need to store energy in case of future famine has not evolved to cope with fast food.

Thus, to handle time today—in the information age, the age of sensory overload—is to handle a new stage in our human history. We need a system that approaches things from the inside out—that is, by looking at what makes human beings tick, both as individuals and as part of a community. Only then can *prioritization, work-life balance, productivity,* and the other time management grails become achievable.

This book, *Cool Time*, helps you develop your system by drawing from three separate streams of established knowledge—(1) project management, (2) psychology, and (3) physiology—in a method that is easy to understand, easy to use, and easy to stick with.

This in turn will give you access to the three key tools of true time management success:

1. inventory,
2. influence, and
3. implementation.

THE THREE I'S

In brief, *inventory* refers to understanding work flow—identifying the types of tasks you are likely to encounter in your future based on what you have encountered in your recent past—and then planning accordingly. This is not as far-fetched as it sounds; in fact, it is part of what makes project management a reliable and sound practice. Taking *inventory* will empower you to predict your day-to-day future, allotting time for regular work, crises, and opportunities, and giving you the strength to defend and spend your time on your terms.

Influence is how you communicate with the people around you—your colleagues, your customers, and your managers—and, more specifically, how you manage their expectations and condition their behavior so their self-interests will coexist with yours. You can influence everyone in your world—including your boss—and actually improve these relationships, while leaving you in greater control over your time and activities. Influence is not manipulation—it's about increased communication and mutual satisfaction, and it has its roots in both project management and psychology.

Implementation is about successfully integrating these new habits in your life, slowly, carefully, and strategically, so that individual improvements and overall *improvement* become permanent, and so that victories are acknowledged along the way. Change does not happen overnight. The New Year's Resolution graveyard is filled with earnest promises for quick self-improvement; however, the human body and mind are not designed for sudden, permanent change, and the same goes for your work community. We need to understand your physiology and that of your neighbors to ensure that new habits take root and thrive.

In short, *Cool Time* establishes the blueprint for effectively managing time in your workplace as well as in your non-work life.

Cool Time will help you experience:

- *An increase in productivity and efficiency: Getting the right things done in the right way.* A cool mind generates clear thoughts and maximizes abilities, both physical and mental. Your ability to focus, to think, to negotiate, and to get the right things done will increase. Through a combination of focus and your new ability to deflect distractions such as e-mail, drop-in visitors, even ambient noise, you will achieve more in less time.

- *A reduction in mental and physical stress or, more precisely, distress.* Distress occurs primarily when what we want to do and what is actually happening come into conflict. It manifests itself physically as discomfort, confusion, illness, and, ultimately, disease. Mental stress derails concentration and forces us to work at reduced capacity. *Cool Time* will help you reduce stress by reinstating control over activities, expectations, and situations.
- *A healthy balance between work and life.* We all know how important it is to counteract the stresses of the workday through exercise and rest, but who has the time for that? Access to these essential contributors to prime functioning and healthy living starts, as you will see, with the enormous benefit that results when we move from *reaction* to *control*.

BENJAMIN FRANKLIN AND *SESAME STREET*

Daylight saving time was first conceived by Benjamin Franklin in 1784 as an economic solution to the problem of living and working in the extended darkness of the winter months. Its acceptance marks a significant development in the relationship between humans and time, since it allowed us to adjust the clocks to suit the needs of business, rather than adjusting business to follow the available daylight.

The introduction of the electric light bulb cemented that dominance over time, and since then, especially within the last fifty years, it has allowed us to become more and more involved with speed: the speed of thought, of communication, of travel, action and of commerce. And, perhaps most importantly, the speed of expectation.

Sesame Street was one of the first TV shows to present learning in a high-speed modular format, using short skits and carefully researched visuals in place of long story lines. The millions of kids who grew up watching *Sesame Street* used a method of thinking that was profoundly different from that of their elders, who had been raised on narratives—stories, radio plays, and books.

These concepts, daylight saving time, the light bulb, and *Sesame Street* are but three milestones along the road of increased human activity, one that has taken us to unprecedented heights and achievements, yet continues to outpace our own internal wiring.

Take, for example, e-mail. Has e-mail remained the efficient global messaging system it was designed to be, or has it become something else to you? For a moment, forget about the spam, the viruses, the patches, the repairs and maintenance issues, and think about how many e-mails would pile up in your in-box if you were to take a week's vacation. Think about the time it takes to go through each one, especially the FYI's, the multigenerational quotes-within-quotes letters, and all those that you're merely cc'd on. Do you have to read them? You won't know if you need to read them until you after you've read them. God forbid if you don't read one and then get called to task about it a week from now.

And you know that going home won't help because the e-mail will continue to arrive. There will always be something else in your in-box to tempt you to stay later and work just a little longer. For some the answer to that is to get a phone or a PDA that can receive e-mail at home. They take it into the bathroom in case something important comes in while they're in the shower, and they set it on the bedside table at night. "At least then," they say, "I can check in and know everything's OK. That way I can go to sleep."

THE SPEED OF EXPECTATION

The *Speed of Expectation* has taken over. We crave the stimulation of the immediate. We need to be in touch, to communicate, to get instant answers. Even if we think we don't like it and would prefer to leave work at work, the addiction to quick stimulation makes it a permanent need.

Occasionally the compounded stresses of this lifestyle lead to rage. Road rage and air rage, for example, have been born out of unrealistic expectations—that we *can* and *must* get to our destination quickly and conveniently. We envision the trip optimistically, with no traffic congestion or delays in mind. Ads for new cars and for air travel always depict clear skies, clear roads, smiling people, and uninterrupted fun. We are conditioned to expect no delays. Traffic jams and airport hold-ups, which frustrate us because they slow us down, release the pent-up frustrations of a life lacking control. Not everyone resorts to outward violence, of course. Some merely internalize their frustrations, to have them later emerge in surprising ways. Take reality TV, for example…

THE ERA OF *SCHADENFREUDE*

Reality TV demonstrates how the age of overload has given birth to the era of *schadenfreude*. *Schadenfreude* is a German term that means "taking pleasure in the misfortunes of others," which is precisely why most people watch reality TV—to observe the expressions on the faces of those who have been voted off the island; whose houses, faces, and lives have been transformed, not always in the way they had hoped; who are trapped, on-screen, in uncomfortable situations. People watch, not to cheer the winners, but to revel in the discomfort of the losers, knowing that for a moment at least, there is someone whose powerless situation we can observe and enjoy. This is how the loss of control manifests itself.

Back in our own lives, speed abounds. In radio broadcasting, for example, dead air is a bad thing. It takes one-third of a second for you, the listener, to pick up on the fact that the radio's silence is longer than it should be, and that someone has missed his cue. We are always consciously and unconsciously aware of the speed of existence, which has resulted in habits and reactions such as:

- Skipping breakfast because there's no time for it in the morning.
- Feeling frustrated by a busy signal on the phone.
- Using a cellphone when driving.
- Hearing news stories about parents "flipping out" on their kids' teachers or coaches.
- Feeling out of touch when the Internet service goes down.
- Wondering why someone you called or e-mailed an hour ago hasn't returned the message.
- Expressing frustration at traffic jams and transit delays.

Perhaps the source of this problem should be traced to the dawn of the information age in 1939.

THE 1939 WORLD'S FAIR, NEW YORK CITY

In 1939 there was a World's Fair in New York City. It was a great time for people to explore the wonders of science and progress. Huge Art Deco pavilions invited eager visitors to experience a future in which sleek, gleaming cars with fins and transparent space bubbles waited to whisk citizens back to suburban homes where robots performed the household chores. By 1985 or maybe 1990, humankind would have to work only two hours a day, leaving the rest of the time for leisure. Or so they said.

The 1939 World's Fair heralded the age of science, the age of speed. But few working professionals today can boast of living the expected two-hour workday, and that's because discovery is never enough. Every time we discover we can do something, we seek a way to do it better (which is good), or faster (which is also good). We then try to find time in an already crammed schedule to fit this new talent in alongside other priorities, which is not so good. As we raise the bar for our abilities, we also raise the bar for our expectations while the platform of time remains fixed. That's why we don't have a two-hour workday. For although we can do more in two hours today than someone in 1939 could have done in an entire day, our human makeup demands that we continue working, and our mental makeup renders us blind to current and past achievements. It's a condition called sensory adaptation.

A good example of this would be the last time you acquired a new computer. Most likely the first half-hour of use was the most fascinating. Everything was so much faster than your old PC—incredibly fast! Yet very quickly you grew used to the speed of the new machine. It became normal, so that you could re-experience how far you'd come only by going back and working on your older, seemingly arthritic PC.

Because sensory adaptation is so common and so natural, I often get asked for the "time management magic bullet," the secret that people think will help them work faster, so they can either get it all done or just get caught up. With a wink, I ask them if they would prefer this solution in aerosol or pill form, since I usually have both in stock, and which, when taken correctly, will make them move in fast-motion, like a movie from the 1920s.

I warn them, however, that it comes with an undesirable side effect: The moment people start working consistently in this new speeded-up mode, the body adjusts, and that new pace becomes the norm. And then they will want to do just one *more* task, to work through lunch, to take on more and more, to never say No. That's when those "magic bullet" customers come back to see me for the extra-strength dose.

The moment we raise the bar of expectation, we forget the limits of our current abilities. Sensory adaptation generates a kind of ergonomic inflation, in which tasks expand to fill the available space, expectation follows, and nobody gains ground.

And it's for that reason that *Cool Time* seeks to provide a solution.

SO IS THIS BOOK FOR YOU?

When I tell people that I teach time management skills, I often get responses such as: "I took a time management course once ...," which is usually followed by the reasons why the course didn't succeed. Others will say, "That stuff wouldn't work at our place—we're pretty unique ..." Though the reasons may vary, most people admit they're still looking for a better way.

If you work for a living, whether in an office or on the road, as part of a company or as a home-based entrepreneur; if you report to others (customers, managers) and/or have others report to you; if you have work that needs to get done and have (or would like to have) a life outside of work, then *Cool Time* is for you.

If you can admit to any of the following symptoms, then *Cool Time* is for you:

- New tasks seem to arrive too quickly before you're finished with current work.
- Things pile up too quickly.
- Meetings happen in place of better things you could be doing.

- Incoming calls and visitors take up too much time.
- Conflicts happen.
- The workspace becomes cluttered.
- Sticky notes litter the walls.
- Your to-do list is unrealistically long.
- You take work home regularly.
- You feel tempted to go into the office on the weekends.
- Your hobbies, nutrition, and exercise goals are falling short.
- You simply have no time.

If you've experienced any of these, then *Cool Time* is for you:

- an increase in your stress level on Sunday afternoon as you anticipate Monday morning
- buildups in stress as the day progresses
- feeling a lack of control
- feeling overwhelmed
- conflicts between family and work
- fatigue, loss of sleep, or trouble sleeping
- resentment toward distractions/politics in the office
- the sense of missing out on some part of life
- feeling burned out
- lapses of memory
- anger toward slower drivers or slow elevators
- feeling and worrying about being out of shape
- feeling like you'll never catch up

It doesn't matter what kind of tools you use—cellphones, PDAs, software calendars (like Microsoft Outlook), or paper-based day planners—because it's not the tool you use, but the technique that counts. It's about creating your own system for keeping in control and feeling in control.

We each have a lot to do each day, and a finite number of days at our disposal. We base much of our self-worth on the tasks and jobs that we're assigned to do, sometimes at the expense of our health, leisure, and family. We actually shouldn't be doing much of what we think we should be doing, and the importance of much of what we think we are doing is artificially inflated in our own minds due to distraction, fatigue, and stress.

The approaches you choose to adopt from this book should become extensions of your own method of living and working. The way in which they help you interact with the people around you will shield you from overload while keeping lines of communication and expectation clear. These approaches must be woven into the existing fabric of your life and become a tangible garment, one that is not only comfortable for you to wear, but one that others can see, touch, and appreciate.

So, let's get started.

CHAPTER 2
YOU ARE HERE: THE HUMAN BODY AND TIME

THE FLOODED BASEMENT

It's a nice day, so you decide to pay a visit to your neighbor. You knock on the door, but there's no answer. Still, you can distinctly hear noise coming from within, a sloshing noise, which is kind of weird, so you venture around to the side of the house for a peek.

Squinting through an open basement window, you see him, up to his knees in water. He is frantically trying to get rid of the flood by using a metal bucket, scooping up as much water as he can, and then pitching it through the window onto your shoes.

"What are you doing?" you ask.

"I've got all this water coming in," he shouts back, "and I can't see where it's coming from."

"Have you tried calling Public Works? Maybe they can turn the water off for you," you suggest.

"I've got no time for that, I've got to see to the water first!" he shouts, and resumes bailing out his flooded basement.

This man is obviously doing the wrong thing. Rather than tackling the source of the problem, he is reacting, desperately trying to clear out the results of the overload. His mind and body have been consumed by a necessity that has overridden clear thought. He is consumed by the urgency of the moment. And all the while, more and more water is coming in.

What would have been the Cool Time thing to do? To go upstairs and use a phone rather than a bucket, to call Public Works first, and maybe rent a pump second.

In this story, the water obviously represents the workloads that seem like an unending and sometimes unpredictable stream. The man with his bucket represents us—our mindset, our efforts, and our tools. The picture is reactive, desperate, and inadequate. But wait a minute. We're all pretty smart people. Why do we often feel that we're trapped in this basement, bailing frantically? Because collectively, we simply have not evolved fast enough to keep up with the stresses of today's world.

RATTLESNAKES AND BEES

We are a product of hundreds of thousands of years of evolution. Our physical bodies, as mentioned in Chapter 1, have not changed much in design in over 50,000 years, yet the tools that shape our lives are for the most part just a couple of decades old. This has a profound impact on how we approach work and time, not because we can do things faster, but because we don't know how to keep the tools themselves, which have their own sense of urgency, under control. The communication they facilitate demands immediate responses.

The deepest and innermost parts of the human brain are dedicated to maintaining and preserving life, for example, breathing and reacting to danger, among other things. One of the human brain's many responsibilities is to enable us to react when we notice flashes of light, bright contrasts, and sudden movements—in other words, changes to the visual field. In the wild, this is extremely useful in helping us to avoid bees, rattlesnakes, and other dangerous creatures by enabling us to perceive the flash of bright color or movement and to get out of the way in a hurry, it is a reflex action.

In the modern world, this ever-alert part of our central nervous system remains constantly on guard, reacting to new "flashes" of our own design. For example, when you're driving, it will pick out the strobe-light flash of a police car or tow truck even in broad daylight, and you will see it first, before all the other visual distractions in front of you. Or if you step off a curb and, out of the corner of your eye, you glimpse a car coming toward you, you will leap back. This self-preservation device delivers a top-priority message to your nervous system to warn you to get out of harm's way.

Now, picture this: You're working away at your desk, and all of a sudden, *bing*! You've got mail! The little symbol tells you there's something new in your mailbox. It wasn't there before, but now it is. What's the first thing you want to do? Answer it, right? It could be important. It could be fun! It's a tantalizing novelty. Most of us cannot resist the lure of the "new mail" icon. The hardwired response of the central nervous system to deal with a new stimulus has now become a conditioned reflex.

Here is another example: You're in the middle of a face-to-face conversation with someone when the phone rings. Your train of thought is derailed briefly as you struggle to override your desire to answer the call, or at least to ignore its persistent ring. You may succeed in not answering it, but the ring has interrupted the momentum of the conversation.

A final example: You arrive at your desk, with the day's schedule clear in your mind. As soon as you sit down, a colleague shows up with an issue that she says is important and needs to be dealt with. You heed the call and before long, all of your planned events of the day get shifted further and further back until your day is a jumbled mess.

In all of these situations, and many others, false urgencies stimulate your innate alert-response trigger, and it's extremely hard to ignore. It's a conditioned reflex—an ancient reflex that responds to modern priorities, which I call *Answerholism*. Once you respond, more time gets wasted, and the slippery slope begins. Just like the neighbor with the flooded basement, the urgency of the immediate overrides our control over our day, and damage occurs.

THE CONDITIONED REFLEX

If you were to sit two people side by side—an Aboriginal hunter, from a remote jungle village, and your real-estate agent—and then place a cellphone between them and make it ring, the hunter would be startled by the sound. That's a reflex. The agent would leap to answer it or to at least check who's calling, preparing her mind for the possibilities and urgencies of the call. If it wasn't her phone, she would probably start to worry about whose phone it was. This concern would override anything else she was thinking about at that moment. That's a conditioned reflex. The need to address the call over all other priorities is Answerholism, an addictive behavior that has less than optimum results.

Before the days of e-mail and voicemail people would return to their office after lunch to find a collection of pink "While You Were Out" memos stuck on a spike on their desk. They would read through these messages and prioritize whom they would call back and when. In that situation, the power of decision rested with the individual's *conscious* mind. That's a big difference. Tangible tools like the pink pieces of paper did not prompt the reactionary central nervous system in the same way the *bing*! of incoming e-mail does. Instead they led to a more conscious and calm thought process. Though the stack of pink papers still meant more tasks to get done, they allowed prioritization to be based on thought, not reflex.

THE FEAR OF THE UNKNOWN

Our desire for self-preservation also translates into a fear of the unknown. For example, our senses sharpen if we walk through a dark forest or down a deserted street at night. But the fear of the unknown strikes in other ways, too. Many people, for example, dislike voicemail. The frustration of not knowing whether a message has reached its recipient is rooted in the fear of the unknown. *Is the person there today? Did she get my message? When will she call back? What does that mean to my projects and priorities?* To that end, some organizations refuse to use voicemail, preferring to remain accessible to their customers by answering every call every time. On both ends of the line, productivity and communication have been hamstrung by the fear of the unknown.

(When properly used, voicemail can be a perfect customer-relations tool, one that proactively manages the fears and concerns of your callers, one that strikes a happy and profitable medium between being accessible to your clients and enabling you to use your time most effectively, simply by choosing the right words to use in your greeting. This will be covered in more detail in Chapter 10.)

THE CIRCADIAN "RHYTHM SECTION"

Another feature of our physical makeup that has a great impact on our perception and use of time is rhythm. Our beating heart is but one of numerous rhythmic patterns in the human body. There are the daily circadian rhythms of sleep and wakefulness, rhythms in speech patterns, energy levels, and in internal chemical and hormonal adjustments. We ride a roller coaster of peaks and valleys, highs and lows. We ride on crests of momentum and energy, and then dip down into ebbs and troughs every ninety minutes. These highs and lows occur throughout the day, buffeting us with changing levels in blood sugar, stress, stamina, and attentiveness, and resulting in a highly variable platform that we call our "selves."

The worst part of the day for most people, for example, is the early to mid-afternoon slot, from 2:00p.m. to 3:30 p.m., a time when the body is at its lowest physical ebb of the entire waking day, and when even the simplest tasks seem to require additional effort. This is due to a sinister combination of circumstances: first, your stomach is busy digesting lunch (assuming you eat lunch, which you should), and, second, an internally generated twelve-hour cycle is busy mirroring the deep-sleep period of 2:00A.M. to 3:30A.M. in which the body is at the lowest ebb of the sleep cycle. This mid-afternoon slog is the period that I call "chocolate time."

WHAT IS IT WITH CHOCOLATE?

Chocolate is a staple of the late-afternoon doldrums. It is high in fat and sugar, which allows the body to quickly convert it into glucose and dissolve it into the bloodstream. It also contains the stimulants caffeine and theobromine, as well as phenylethylamine, which react with dopamine to release endorphins from the pleasure center of the brain—the same endorphins that are released during times of emotional pleasure. This is why so many cultures equate chocolate with sex (think Valentine's Day). Some even say chocolate is better.

As if these cycles and troughs weren't enough, we humans have another impediment to efficiency, which is our built-in daily downward spiral—our metabolic peaks and valleys gradually lower as the day goes on. For most people, whether they want to admit it or not, mornings are the period of highest energy and alertness, and it goes downhill from there.

Figure 2.1: This line represents our typical metabolic roller coaster of blood sugar and energy levels. We spend our days on a downward spiral toward sleep. However, adequate regular nutrition and balance can help level out the peaks and troughs quite significantly.

Biologically, we are a light-loving species. Our minds and metabolisms react to the changes in light as night turns to day by releasing stimulant hormones such as serotonin (a sleep inhibitor) and cortisol (a stress hormone) into the bloodstream to counteract the effects of melatonin, which it introduced the evening before to get us to go to sleep.

This daily rhythm is called *circadian*, from the Latin words *circa* (around) and *dian* (day). Nature attuned us as hunter-gatherers to be alert first thing in the morning (when food would be more plentiful) and sleepy at night (because darkness gives protection from predators and motionlessness is protection from injury).

Most people in the Western working world and, statistically, the majority of people you interact with will follow this circadian rhythm, with mornings (between 9:00A.M. and 12:00P.M.) being the time for productive, cerebral activities, and afternoons best suited for less challenging tasks.

STRIKE WHILE THE COFFEE IS HOT

The best time to communicate important information to people is between 9:00A.M. and 9:30A.M. That's when the combined influences of light, caffeine, and the activity of traveling to work yield the greatest alertness for all involved. Schedule your meetings for 9:00A.M. sharp, and get your most important concepts out on the table within the first thirty minutes.

SLEEP, PERCHANCE TO DREAM

Most of us also operate in sleep deficit. Current studies show that the average North American adult needs between eight and ten hours of sleep per night.[1] Some might need less, but an easy way to determine if you're getting enough sleep is this: If you need an alarm clock to wake up in the morning, that means you are not waking up naturally, which means your sleep cycle isn't in tune with your day. If you wake up Monday morning having had one hour of sleep less than you need, then you are in sleep deficit. If the same thing happens on Tuesday, Wednesday, and Thursday, by the time you get to Friday, you're short five hours of sleep. Then, by trying to compensate by sleeping in on Saturday morning, you throw off your rhythm even further. (The best solution is to get up at the same time every day, and go to bed at the same time every night.)

---

1 National Sleep Foundation (www.Sleepfoundation.org).

Sleep deficit is another example of the disparity between our perceptions of our actions and abilities within time and the reality. We are fighting battles with ourselves, physically, chemically, emotionally, and intellectually every second of the day.

By the way, there is a better solution to sleep deficit than merely going to bed earlier, and that's to introduce higher quality sleep more quickly through the proper use of "downtime." We'll cover this in Chapter 12.

THE CIRCULAR WORLD

Meanwhile, the rotations of days, nights, seasons, tides, and the moon continue without fail. The plants and trees of the world breathe and release carbon dioxide every twenty-four hours, while large-scale weather patterns ferry moisture, cold, and warmth from one part of the globe to another. The planet itself seems to be breathing, living, and playing to its own vast cadence.

This innate sense of rhythm then influences our perception of time, so that it too seems to have a rhythmic or circular pattern. Clocks repeat the same numbers every twelve hours. We have only seven days of the week, so each comes around regularly. New Year's Day also comes around once a year, the Olympic Games every four years, and so on. Circularity allows society to structure itself with predictability and standardization. It would be extremely difficult for any society to continue without it. But all that next Tuesday has in common with this Tuesday is its name, nothing more.

Our vernacular is full of phrases that enliven time and make it a real commodity. Expressions such as "I haven't got the time," or "Time flies," or "Where did the day go?" give time an elasticity that doesn't exist. We talk about people "wasting time," "spending time," "killing time," "managing time," as if it were a substance to be bought, sold, and reused. Everyone knows these are harmless sayings, but they, too, place the blame and the responsibility for change squarely on the shoulders of time itself. We have convinced ourselves that we could have, or should have, or actually do have control over time, and we find ourselves mystified when the truth comes out.

Though it is convenient to match our calendar with the annual rhythms of the seasons, and to objectify time as a tangible object, we should take more care to see ourselves as we really are—marching in a straight line, advancing along our own finite section of an eternal straight line like ants on a ruler.

OSMOSIS AND FOOTBALL IN THE WORKPLACE

Humans are also by nature social creatures, so we tend to invite and enjoy conversation, distraction, and mental stimulation: the joke-of-the-day e-mail from a friend, the water-cooler chat, a brief stint of surfing the web. These things can be effective in enlivening the day and providing a few moments of leisure, but they do come with a price, for after they have passed, the work still remains to be done, and we are then forced to stay late, take work home, or make other sacrifices to catch up.

Furthermore, as products of our Western education system, most of us are trained in a skill and then join the workforce. We continue to learn though training and professional development courses, as well as practical experience, hopefully building a stable career and putting food on the table. However, another, more sinister type of learning also happens. While we integrate ourselves into the corporate culture of the company, we start to adopt the habits and norms of our peers, including many latent, long-established time inefficiencies that are passed on through osmosis.

It takes us by surprise, therefore, when we learn for the first time that most people "work" for only about one-third of the hours that they spend "at work," meaning they actually will get only three hours of measurable work done in an eight- or nine-hour day.[2] Though this at first seems to be an affront to our ambitions, it doesn't actually refer to a lack of dedication or drive. The average business day is full of productivity roadblocks such as meetings, e-mail, and drop-in visitors, conflicts and staff issues, technological problems and crises, all of which, though they may be considered as part of the work for which we are being paid, occur in irregular and

---

2 James P. Lewis, *Mastering Project Management* (New York: McGraw-Hill, 1998), p. 165.

unpredictable ways, breaking up the momentum of work and delaying tasks on our calendar. The difference between how much we think we've done and how much work we have actually achieved is surprising.

But three hours? That's a small fraction of a day to be counted as productive work in the purest sense of the word. It's like taking a stopwatch to a football game. Over the course of a four-hour game, between the downs, the line changes, and the time-outs, the ball is actually only in play for about twenty minutes—a very small segment of the game's entire span.

Numerous polls of North American professionals have revealed that for many, during the course of a workday, these things happen:

- 25 percent of people's time is spent doing actual work
- 15 percent of the day is spent responding to e-mail and voicemail
- 15 percent of the day is spent on the phone
- 20 percent of the day is spent in meetings and conversations
- 25 percent of the day is spent preparing for those meetings or dealing with the follow-up

The fact that such a relatively small amount of the workday is spent doing actual planned work is often overlooked until someone is called upon to estimate the delivery date of a project. In an attempt to please a potential new client, you, your boss, or your salesperson might say, "We can have that to you by Thursday." In fact, if you had nothing else to do, and could work on this client's needs exclusively for eight uninterrupted hours a day, you probably could have it ready for Thursday. But that's being way too optimistic, and that's where the problems happen. We have to be realistic, and even a little bit pessimistic. We don't know what other crises might happen between now and Thursday, but we can count on a few simple truths:

- Things always take longer than you think, and a lot longer than you hope.
- If someone asks you to do something and includes the word "just," as in "Can you just …?" you're already in trouble.

- There'll never be a perfect time to get it done.
- No matter how many good things you do for a person, he'll always remember (and talk about) the one bad thing that happened.

WATER IN THE BUCKET

This chapter started with the story of a man and his bucket. Let's have a last look at that bucket. A bucket can hold a fixed amount of water. Once the bucket is filled to the brim, you can try to pour more water in, but an equal amount will have to come back out. It just cannot hold any more.

Now let this bucket represent a fixed amount of time. We each have access to twenty-four hours a day, but we can't borrow any time from previous days, nor can we ask for repeats or advances. These twenty-four-hour days come and go, regularly and unfailingly. The day is fixed in length. It is the primary working tool of our existence.

Many people start off their days with the best intentions, planning what they will do and in which order, yet things quickly start to unravel as urgencies of all sorts start to occur. The day's schedule, which was probably already full of planned tasks, now starts to overflow. People get stressed, and they work through lunch and stay late to try to get back on top of things. They expand and distort their working day in order to keep up with the overflow of work. They wish for more hours in a day, or for time to freeze, just until they're caught up. They're on a quest for more time—that bigger bucket. The problem is that even with a bigger bucket, they'll still end up working twice as hard to move half as much water.

The trick to time management, just like the trick to dealing with a flooded basement, is in learning how to use your bucket rather than trying to find a bigger one. Effective time management means using the right strategy, not making more work hours available or working twice as fast or twice as hard. Effective time managers do not feel an obsessive need to fill every moment with productive work—quite the opposite. They envision and enact a rational plan that includes time for the expected, the unexpected, and the opportunities so that in the end, every moment can be used properly and profitably. They balance priorities, and they manage the needs of their colleagues. They recognize and accept that the in-box will never be empty. They go home at the end of the day knowing that they have done good work and that they will do more tomorrow.

They understand that control makes the difference. It paves the way for influence, productivity, and satisfaction. So let's now start on the Cool Time path to success by first taking inventory.

CHAPTER 3
INVENTORY AND ITS ROLE IN PREDICTING THE FUTURE

THE ART OF WAR

The Art of War is a manual of military strategy written by the Chinese general Sun Tzu over 2,000 years ago. In it he affirms that every battle is won or lost before it is even started: The victorious commander understands and respects his enemy, and becomes aware of the strengths and weaknesses of both sides, primarily by taking a higher perspective, being able to see the entire landscape, including his own forces, the enemy's forces, and all other circumstances that may affect the outcome.

Time is your battlefield. Your talents and ambitions comprise your army and everyone else in your world occupies the opposing camp. Taking inventory of your assets and liabilities within time means looking backwards, taking stock, and then moving forward with a solid yet flexible plan, one that can influence others and be implemented practically. This is where the wisdom of project management comes in.

A CRASH COURSE IN PROJECT MANAGEMENT

Project management has been around as a formalized school of thought and study since the 1950s. It emphasizes the importance of planning, communication, performance, and review. It starts with a higher-level perspective of a project, and then breaks it down to the smallest reasonable components. Project management forces you to visualize a project from beginning to end. It allows you to plan for contingencies and revisions, and replaces the traditional "seat-of-the-pants" approach with an organized, accountable agenda.

The Project Management Institute (www.pmi.org) is an authority on project management, and publishes a work known as the *Project Management Body of Knowledge* (PMBOK). The intent of the PM-BOK is to assist project managers everywhere, regardless of their experience, by providing a standard and a logical plan for the successful completion of projects.

Planning

Initiation

Control

Execution

Closure

Figure 3.1: The *Project Management Body of Knowledge* identifies five phases in the life of a typical project.

- *Initiation*: In this phase, the project is conceived and assessed as viable or not; ideas are formulated; and the expected results and timeline are first considered.
- *Planning*: A significant amount of time on the project—sometimes most of it—is spent here. Every detail of the project is accounted for, including possible failures, contingencies, estimated times for completion of each part, and budget and resource estimates.
- *Execution*: The project gets underway, people start to work on the project, and momentum begins.
- *Control*: The work of the project is performed, while the project manager oversees and updates the plan and communicates progress and changes to all involved.

- *Closure*: Once the project is completed, the project teams are broken up, final accounting is done, and things are cleaned up and put away.

The project is summarized and guided by a *project plan*, a document that lays out tasks and their respective time lines throughout the life of the project. Far from being a static document, the project plan remains flexible, a living, breathing thing, that can adapt to changes while still allowing the project to move ahead.

Though no project manager has a crystal ball to predict how things will pan out in the future, she can look back into the past, through research, analysis, and consultation with experts and mentors to know, within reason, what to expect.

A WEDDING: PROJECT MANAGEMENT WITH CAKE AT THE END

Even if you've never studied project management, if you've been involved in planning a wedding, you know what it's about—fixed budgets, fixed time lines, inexperience, and lots of pressure. That's why many wedding planners hand out guidebooks with titles such as *What to Do When Planning Your Wedding*. It's project management for the uninitiated.

In short, project management makes everything as clear as possible and envisions all aspects of the project before they happen. It does not necessarily make a project effortless, but its principles and rules ensure that work and resources are properly guided. The planning phase allows for an educated degree of foresight (inventory), the control phase ensures clear communication and instruction (influence), and together they create a road map to help keep the project on course (implementation).

CHAPTER 3

WHAT DOES THAT HAVE TO DO WITH TIME MANAGEMENT?

Everything! Project management is central to successful time management since everything you undertake is a project in one way or another. Each day is a project, as are the weeks, months, jobs, vacations, and events that make up your life. Project management provides lessons that are key to the successful use of time. For example:

- *The legitimacy of planning*: Taking time to create a practical, flexible, workable action plan gives you a realistic structure for the day, and a tangible tool for negotiation, delegation, and influence.
- *The importance of control*: Allowing yourself time to update your daily project plan and communicate it to others as the day unfolds ensures clarity of thought and action in the face of oncoming tasks and stress.
- *Closure: Taking the time to follow up*: People who jump from task to task without taking a moment to schedule follow-up activities are doomed to forget something. Closure on a task-by-task basis ensures that nothing falls into the cracks. Closure on a day-by-day basis ensures continuous control and improvement.
- *The value of learning from the past in predicting the future*: People often say, "I cannot use time management techniques because every day is too different." However, if you were to step back and observe work patterns over longer periods, say, a month, a quarter, a year, or five years, certain configurations would emerge—patterns that empower you to predict the future and control events to a far greater degree than you'd originally thought. This is exactly what we'll discuss on page 30.

THE CRITICAL PATH

Another project management term that has implications in time management is the *critical path*, which is defined as the shortest possible time line by which all component tasks of a project can be completed. Like the carriages on a train, they are rigid and locked together, so that if any one of the tasks is delayed by a day or even a few hours, each successive task will have to move with it, and the project will be late or over budget.

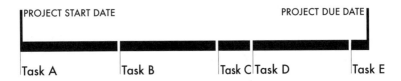

Figure 3.2: Working to the critical path: No room for the unexpected.

A wise project manager does not want to be on the critical path. However, she knows it is wise to identify it, so as to be able to plan backwards from the due date, and then factor in some extra time to allow for the unexpected. For example, a task that might take two days of actual labor will be planned as needing three, so that when something unexpected happens, a delay of even an entire day will not affect the project.

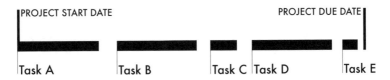

Figure 3.3: Working off the critical path is much healthier and more realistic. Note the gaps between the tasks.

WHAT DOES THE CRITICAL PATH HAVE TO DO WITH TIME MANAGEMENT?

Many people work to a critical path every day. Meetings are booked back-to-back, projects and to-do lists fill the schedule to such a degree that even taking a lunch break becomes out of the question. The pressure of getting everything done forces people to line up tasks one after the other, like a never-ending freight train, and things inevitably run over time.

Cool Time changes all that. Once we build our task inventory, we will apply it to build a new type of daily project plan called the *I-Beam Agenda*. As a wise project manager, you will then be able to identify your critical path and steer away from it.

THE HOOVER DAM

The Hoover Dam, on the Arizona–Nevada border, stands as one of the greatest engineering marvels of the twentieth century. It is a shining example of successful project management. In fact, it helped develop many of the techniques still used in project management and construction today, from just-in-time delivery of materials to the development of the hard hat. Frank Crowe, the dam's project manager, was able to bring the project in two years early, which was doubly impressive, given that he faced a hefty fine for each day the project ran over.

A fascinating fact about this huge structure is that it's not actually attached to anything! That monstrous dam is held against the canyon walls by the pressure of the water itself. As the engineers point out, it has to have room to expand and contract with the climate of the desert and to move with the tectonics of the Earth. If it were fixed rigidly, it would destroy itself. It demonstrates perfectly how flexibility is the key to strength.

TAKING INVENTORY

People often say their problem with time management is that they can't plan for the unknown. "I don't know what's going to happen to-day," they say, "and even if I plan my day, there's always something that comes along that throws all my plans out the window." Well, actually, there's a lot we can do to predict and influence the future, and a lot we can do to ensure we get the right things done when and how we want. It starts by taking inventory, and for that, let's have a quick look inside your favorite restaurant.

How does a restaurant chef know how much beef to buy per week? How much fish? How many pounds of strawberries? With experience and review, he can observe the eating habits and traffic patterns of his customers, and can expect, with 90 percent accuracy, that Friday lunch-times and Sunday dinners will be the busiest, and that Wednesdays are the most popular days for fish. He can buy accordingly (inventory) and then influence the diners' choices by creating a pleasing menu. The economics of the restaurant business do not allow for wasted food, so an effective future depends on learning from the past.

Unless you've been at your current job for less than five days, you too have a good sense of the types of tasks that you face in your day. These can be categorized into two types—predictable, and what I call "expectable"—or, in other words, the normal stuff that you *know* is going to happen and the other stuff that just might happen. The goal of taking inventory is to ensure enough time is reserved for each of these types of tasks.

Let's clarify further: Predictable tasks are the ones you expect on a daily basis. These may include:

- regularly scheduled meetings
- preparing your store, department, or office to open for business
- phone calls
- e-mail
- office interaction and chat
- focused, self-directed work
- administration

You might have others to add to this list depending on your particular job. They might include:

- traveling to a customer location
- dealing face-to-face with customers
- giving presentations

It's up to you to identify the predictable tasks specific to your work. The point is, whatever type of job you have, they're the activities that you know will happen on a given day, but not necessarily at a fixed time. They're just part of what makes up "work."

But let's stop and look at them a little more closely before moving on to the second category, the expectables.

What do you know about your predictable tasks? If someone was to ask you, "On any given day, how many meetings do you actually attend? How many phone calls do you make and take? How many e-mails do you deal with?" you'd probably shrug your shoulders and say, "It depends on the day." If you were pressed harder for an answer, what would it be? Two meetings a day? Four? Six? Do you make and take twenty phone calls a day or 200? Maybe then you could come up with a reasonable number. Now, how long does each of these tasks take? How long is the average meeting? How long is the average phone call? How long do you spend reading and responding to each e-mail? Perhaps Mondays are different from Fridays in terms of what you have to do, and certainly one phone call or e-mail will differ from the next. But the point is, these are the activities that fill up our days. We know they're going to happen, yet they still occur in an uncontrolled manner.

And "uncontrolled" is one thing we want to avoid since once we enter the "uncontrolled zone," we lose track of time.

THE UNBEARABLE LIGHTNESS OF BEING UNCONTROLLED

Have you ever been introduced to someone new only to forget his name five minutes later? This is an example of being trapped in an uncontrolled moment. It's because the actions involved during a formal introduction require so much presence of mind—the handshake, the smile, the posture, the formalities involved in meeting—that any extra information, such as the person's name, goes skipping off the surface of our short-term memory like a pebble on a lake. We are not in control.

The trick is to change your approach from reactive to proactive. As you extend your hand for a handshake, remind yourself that memorization must now occur. This requires no change in your outward behavior, no need to shake hands more aggressively; it simply sets the stage for the crucial next few seconds of social interaction.

Make sure you hear the person's name, and then use word association immediately to tie the name to an icon or image in your mind. Does he look vaguely like a celebrity? Someone you went to

school with? You certainly don't have to reveal the specific association to the person; in fact it's wise to keep that information entirely to
yourself, but it guarantees an easy way to remember a name for the
duration of the conversation.

The point of this name-remembering lesson is not the word-
association trick itself, but to *remember* to do it when the time comes.
Once you remember to do the word association, you will have transformed that interaction from an uncontrolled one to a proactive one,
and that's what we want to achieve for the entire workday—control.

If you take the time now to quantify how long your predictable
tasks will take you on a given day, based on your past experience, you
can predict with reasonable certainty how many hours per day must
be set aside for them in the future. You know that there will be phone
calls, e-mail, and meetings next Monday, so why not reserve the time
for them now?

You don't have to get down to exact numbers, minutes, and seconds (we don't need to get obsessive here), but it's just like keeping a
household budget. You have to understand your expenses in order to
manage your purchases. For example, you might recognize that on a
given day:

- You make and receive roughly ten phone calls.
- The average duration of a phone call is six minutes.
- You often have two longer calls each day of fifteen minutes each.
- The total daily inventory of calls is ninety minutes.
- You write and receive twenty e-mails.
- The time it takes you to handle each e-mail is five minutes.
- The total daily inventory of e-mails is 100 minutes.
- You attend two meetings (both formal and casual meetings).
- The average duration of a formal meeting is sixty minutes.
- The average duration of a casual meeting is fifteen minutes.
- The total daily inventory of meetings is seventy-five minutes.

THE VOLUME OF A DAY

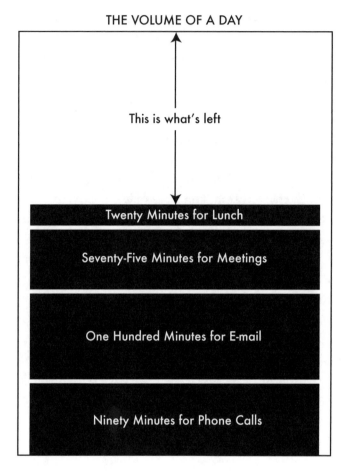

Figure 3.4: This is generally how much time you have to allow for the regular activities of the day.

Suppose also that your workday is from 8:00a.m. to 5:00p.m., a total of nine hours. Well, then, for this given day, we can already predict that over four and a half hours need to be reserved for e-mail, phone calls, and meetings.

"Yes, but," you say, "I can't tell if I will be on the phone for a predictable number of minutes. Things are just way too busy for that—there's no consistency!"

To which I respond, "Just think back." Remember yesterday, the day before, the day before that, and back as far as you want to. You likely see some regular daily volumes of activity that *can* be quantified. What might be obscuring the view, however, is that these predictable events occur somewhat randomly throughout the day. Your next task, once you've identified both the predictable and expectable tasks, will be to arrange them into a more convenient sequence, using the power of influence as your chief weapon.

Expectable Tasks

Expect the unexpected. This other category of tasks consists of the things that come at you from left field and derail all of your other neat plans. Most people refer to them as "crises," and they are the reason other time management approaches fail. It's easy to plan for what you know is coming, but what about what you can't foresee? My point is, if an activity happens occasionally, and can happen again, then it should not be viewed as a "crisis" but as an "expectable event." This is important, since an event that is expected, even if not desired, can be integrated into a time management plan, whereas one that we "just hope won't happen," tends to get forgotten about until it's too late.

Examples of what others would define as a crisis but that I would define as "expectable" might include: Your manager drops an additional task onto your desk; a colleague calls in sick; an unhappy customer shows up demanding satisfaction; a defective product is returned; the CEO arrives unexpectedly from head office. These are things that have happened before, and as unwelcome as they may be, they will likely happen again. Though you can't predict *when*, your experience will give good insight into the odds of one happening, which in project management terms is a sound estimation and planning technique.

The main thing to remember is that by identifying and planning for the predictable tasks we spoke of earlier, as well as the less frequent, less desirable "expectable" tasks of your day, you are not adding more to your plate; you are being realistic and taking stock of the numerous tasks you face on a given day that are usually so split up that they become a blur. You are allotting the time for them in advance and allowing them to become parts of your project plan, rather than simply reacting to them when they happen. That's control.

THE VOLUME OF A DAY

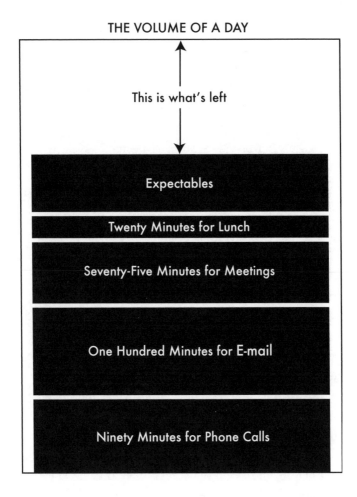

This is what's left

Expectables

Twenty Minutes for Lunch

Seventy-Five Minutes for Meetings

One Hundred Minutes for E-mail

Ninety Minutes for Phone Calls

Figure 3.5: This is what you'll have to allow to include the expected types of activity.

THE POWER OF THE RESERVED ACTIVITY

Think of the number of times you've set out somewhere, perhaps to a shopping mall or downtown, only to find your plans delayed while you circle the block or cruise the parking lot looking for a space. It takes the momentum out of your trip, at least for a short while; yet parking is something we usually don't think about until we arrive. Wouldn't it be nice to have a series of permanent, personal parking spaces at all of our regular destinations to just slide into whenever we want? This would to be spent on tasks rather than on travel.

In the context of your busy workday, that's what you can do when you schedule the results of your inventory and actually put them into your calendar, every day, as reserved activities. Most people schedule only the unique activities, such as a specific meeting or a dental appointment, and that's where the problems start. Suppose a colleague calls you up and says, "We need to meet next Tuesday. What does your day look like?" (Worse, he simply looks up your calendar on the shared network calendar system and books the meeting on your behalf.) The odds are that your schedule for next Tuesday will show only the unique items, leaving the rest of the day deceptively empty.

However, if you have scheduled your predictable and expectable activities as daily reserved events, Tuesday's calendar will clearly show a block of time put aside for the work of the day. This reserved block will not swallow 100 percent of the day, as Figure 3.6 (below) shows. There will still be time available to meet with your colleague. However, the power of the reserved activity helps ensure that even those days you haven't thought much about yet are already well prepared for the work to come.

7:00 A.M.					
8:00 A.M.					
9:00 A.M.	Phone Calls	Phone Calls	Phone Calls	Phone Calls	Phone Calls
10:00 A.M.	E-mail	E-mail	E-mail	E-mail	E-mail
11:00 A.M.					
12:00 P.M.	Lunch	Lunch	Lunch	Lunch	Lunch
1:00 P.M.	Meetings	Meetings	Meetings	Meetings	Meetings
2:00 P.M.					
3:00 P.M.	Expectables	Expectables	Expectables	Expectables	Expectables
4:00 P.M.					
5:00 P.M.					
6:00 P.M.					

Figure 3.6: It doesn't mean you're free to meet with your colleague only between 3:30 P.M. and 5:00 P.M. The components can be moved around to suit your needs, as the next section, "From Blocks to Bits" describes. But at least you and he each know how much time you can realistically spare.

If you use software such as Microsoft Outlook or ACT! to schedule your day, then setting an activity as "Reserved" on a recurring basis is easy. But even if you use a paper day planner, you can mark off these recurring activities with a pencil.

FROM BLOCKS TO BITS

Obviously, your day will not end up with all of your predictable and expectable activities happening in one neat, uninterrupted block. The objective of the inventory, and of scheduling the results as reserved activities, is to allot the appropriate number of minutes and hours to the tasks you know will happen. You are reserving your parking spaces in advance. As your day unfolds, the activities will happen as they happen, but at least you will be ready for them. And then, in Chapter 4 you will refine these allotted minutes by using the I-Beam Agenda to create more functional blocks of time and, in later chapters, you will learn how to influence your colleagues and clients to play along.

ANNUAL PATTERNS

Inventory is not only a tool for daily activities. It also helps you step back and identify the patterns and events that shape the year so you can avoid getting taken by surprise. For some this includes creating a wall chart that identifies:

- peak business periods
- quiet business periods
- statutory holidays
- employee vacations
- spring break
- Christmas/holiday season
- all other long-term events that will have an impact on their time plans

THE BENEFITS OF PLANNING

If you look back at the five phases of project management at the start of this chapter, you'll notice that the planning phase seems very large. No matter how long a project's life is, much time has to be given to planning, which scares people.

But planning is *part* of a project, not a precursor to getting started, and a project manager recognizes this. The old expression goes, "If you fail to plan, you plan to fail," but I prefer the words of Abraham Lincoln, who said, "If you give me six hours to chop down a tree, I'll spend four sharpening my axe." You must be ready before you start.

Taking the time up front to plan your day gives you the power to:

- identify and steer away from the critical path
- allow for the predictable and expectable tasks
- build a workable project plan
- build a platform for mental focus and commitment
- build a tool for negotiation and influence
- set in place a tradition of continuous improvement ...

and still have time and energy for a life.

CHAPTER 4
THE I-BEAM AGENDA: APPLYING INVENTORY AND STRUCTURE

The I-Beam Agenda takes the principles of inventory and project management and fits them into the workday to ensure tasks are being addressed and prioritized in their proper order, and to ensure also that tools for influence (negotiation, communication, and defense) take shape. This chapter describes the basic I-Beam Agenda principles and shows how to create the most proactive and flexible schedule possible. Chapter 6 identifies modules that you can add to your I-Beam Agenda to infuse the day with maximum potential.

HOW DOES IT WORK?
The I-Beam Agenda brackets each day with short planning and review sessions, linked by a control phase (thus the I-Beam shape).

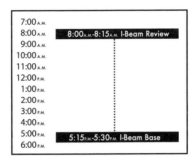

Figure 4.1: The I-Beam Agenda

The top of the I-Beam, called the I-Beam Review, is where you plan *realistically* and *pragmatically* for the day to come. This is not the same as simply reading your calendar when you arrive at work, or going through a mental list of appointments as you drive in—that's reactive. People who do that find their day getting out of control by 11:00a.m. The fifteen-minute I-Beam Review is an exercise in proactive project planning in which you tell your calendar what you're going to do.

The middle of the I-Beam, represented by the dotted line, is the "spine" of your day, during which you have your meetings, do your work, take your breaks, perform your tasks, and so on. This spine represents the control phase of project management, in which we recognize that things will change and veer off course from our original plan, and that as wise project managers, it's our responsibility to keep the hand on the tiller and modify and update the plan accordingly to ensure that everyone, including ourselves, remains up to speed.

The bottom of the I-Beam, the I-Beam Base, allows for closure—for two reviews of the day just past: (1) task summation and (2) continual improvement. Let's have a look at each of these in detail.

THE TOP OF THE I-BEAM: THE I-BEAM REVIEW

STORYBOARDING

Part of the major effort that goes into the creation of a movie is a process called storyboarding, in which film directors hire talented storyboard artists to create a comic-strip version of the film. Though the public seldom sees this artwork, it helps everyone on the production team to visualize the story, anticipate problems, and prepare solutions. All involved want to make sure they know as much about themselves and the project as possible. They recognize the value of being completely in control before heading out to "do battle," even if it takes time to do this.

A fifteen-minute I-Beam Review in the morning is the beginning of your battle plan. This is where you:

- review your newest inbound e-mail and voicemails and schedule responses accordingly
- prepare your daily outbound voicemail greeting, your primary defense against interruption that can still satisfy the needs of the callers
- adjust the block of time reserved for predictable and expectable tasks to fit with the other demands of the day
- prioritize your currently known tasks and assign your highest-priority task to your Keystone Time (Keystone Time is a block of mostly undisturbed time, in which the most important work of the day actually gets done. It will be described fully in Chapter 6.
- delegate whatever can be delegated
- ensure your calendar (project plan) is up-to-date on screen or on paper
- think through and anticipate travel plans
- ensure adequate communication (huddles) with the boss
- put the tasks of the day in perspective to ensure no time is spent on unnecessary or less valuable activities

Think back to the description of what has happened to us since the 1939 World's Fair. The pace of life and the speed of information flow have increased exponentially, forcing us to continually raise the bar of our own expectations. This has forced us into a reactive mode, in which we are compelled to respond to rather than control external stimuli. In that sense, the schedule owns *us*. An I-Beam Review, by contrast, uses techniques that ensure we benefit from prediction and planning rather than suffer under the yoke of reaction.

The I-Beam Review also makes things real, since vague notions make weak bargaining chips. If you rely on a prioritization system that is entirely in your head—a mental list of to-do's and appointments—*you* may know where you're going, but no one else will. This makes for a very ineffective bargaining position when conflicting tasks are sent your way. When people ask you to take on a new task, they seldom stop to think about what you've already got planned that morning, and they certainly will not be inclined to second-guess their own need to talk to you. A tangible agenda, on the other hand, is a communications tool that becomes useful for negotiating workloads and conflicts, and influencing your requestors.

Also, a casual list, whether in your head or informally jotted down, is prone to being overruled when change happens. As external events influence your day's project plan, your short-term memory is forced into overload, and if that's where you keep your schedule, you will be less able to think and prioritize clearly. By contrast, when the items that comprise your current agenda are recorded and set aside some-where physical, your mind is free to deal fully with new challenges.

So, What Should You Do During the I-Beam Review?

First, reserve the time for the review itself. Make it a standard, recurring activity first thing every morning. Let everyone know that you're not actually open for business yet. Even after you have arrived at your of-fice, even if you work from home, the day cannot begin until you have reviewed and updated your project plan. There is an all-too-human tendency for people to expect you to be available the moment they see you, even if you haven't sat down yet. Not only should you be able to find time to take off your coat and get a coffee, but those first ten to fifteen minutes must also be defended as "not-yet-open-for-business" time. Think, once again, of the chef at a restaurant. There is much to be done before opening the doors to paying customers.

Granted, establishing I-Beam Review time can be tricky when you first start out because people are used to talking with you the moment they see you. But we'll cover that in Chapters 5 and 14. It's essential to condition your people to understand your new ways of doing things and to learn what's in it for them to play along. Just because you have been doing things in a certain way in the past doesn't mean you can't change now. It's all in how you communicate it to them.

Second, identify fixed appointments and be brutally realistic about durations and travel times. Though we will learn (in Chapter 8) how to keep meetings and discussions short and effective, some things will always take longer than we'd like, and time must be reserved for this. Simply stacking tasks back-to-back on your agenda won't make them any easier. Cool Time demands practical realism, not adherence to the critical path.

Third, break up the block of time reserved for the predictable and unexpected tasks (see Figure 3.6, page 37) and assign them appropriately throughout the day. As we discuss in Chapter 6, a block of time reserved for returning phone calls and e-mails is far more productive than dealing with them as they arrive. Assign blocks as appropriate for the morning and afternoon. Ditto for your keystone time.

Fourth, change today's to-do's into appointments. To-do's, those tasks that occupy a list at the edge of your calendar, are dangerous. They have to get done *sometime*, but because they each lack a specific start or end time, it is too easy to overlook their duration, which is a fatal mistake because even the smallest to-do task will take more of your time than you'd expect.

Move them off the to-do list and directly onto your calendar as appointments.

For example, what if each of the ten to-do's on your list required fifteen minutes to complete? If you were to schedule each one of them as a fixed appointment in your calendar, they would add up to 150 minutes (two and a half hours), which would fill your afternoon up pretty quickly. That may not be great news, but the point is that if they really *have* to get done, then *are they worthy of promotion from a to-do to an appointment for today's schedule?* If they are, then take them off the to-do list and put them on the calendar (or write them, if you're using a paper planner). Do what you have to do to make them real.

This may appear trivial at first glance, but it goes a long way toward ensuring that you deal with the work that has to get done, while protecting your time against intrusions and the false urgency that newly arrived requests may present.

In Chapter 9 we discuss how to "box" an event, such as a phone call, meeting, or task so that it lasts a specific amount of time, say, five minutes, rather than allowing it to unfold spontaneously and in an uncontrolled way. With that skill in place, you will be able to more realistically plan the durations of these to-do's as they become appointments.

Fifth, schedule time for lunch. Nutrition and refreshment are essential for productivity and success. (See Chapter 12.) Make your lunchtime—even if it's just twenty minutes—sacrosanct.

Sixth, schedule for opportunity time. This is time reserved for the truly unexpected and is the doorway to continued success. (See Chapter 6.)

The I-Beam Review sets your day on a positive, realistic course. It liberates your mind from having to make logistical decisions on the spot, and also puts you in a great position to handle both the expected and the unexpected. Yes, it takes fifteen minutes of your day to do this, but it means that the rest of your working day remains under total Cool control.

THE MIDDLE OF THE I-BEAM

The I-Beam Agenda's spine plays a crucial role in keeping things up-to-date and under control.

We saw in Chapter 3 how a project plan stays flexible and current as the project progresses. So should your daily activities. Imagine being captain of a large freighter as it moves across the water, facing tides, wind, and waves. It would be foolish to set a course, lock the tiller, and then leave the bridge with no one in command. The ship would be soon influenced by those outside forces and would start to drift. Keeping on course requires constant vigilance, and so it is with your day. As the priorities of your day move and change, so should your schedule be updated—physically edited to reflect your new "position."

Though regular updates of your day-plan may seem like extra work, the more you get into the habit of doing this, in combination with planning at the beginning and end of each day using the I-Beam Agenda, the easier it will be to handle and prioritize change, since your creative mind already has 80 percent of your day under control. Second, change will happen anyway, and it is the person who is prepared who has the greater chance of handling it successfully than the person who banks on "winging it."

Each task you choose, each decision you make, each new challenge that comes your way should find its proper place on your living, breathing project plan. At all times it's essential to keep your hand on that tiller.

THE I-BEAM BASE

The fifteen minutes invested at the start of the day as part of the I-Beam Review is best complemented by fifteen minutes at the end of the day for post-planning.

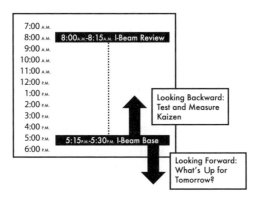

Figure 4.2: The I-Beam Base has two project management–related roles: closure and continual improvement.

Great athletes stay great by returning to the practice area immediately after winning a tournament. Successful television sitcom stars stay fresh by playing at small clubs. Great sales professionals stay successful by asking their clients what they liked and didn't like about their last sales experience. It's constant review, test and measure, continual improvement.

The base of the I-Beam provides an opportunity to advance your career by leaps and bounds by doing something that most people seldom have the time or the inclination to do. That's to review, in the name of follow-through and improvement. For many people just getting through the day is an achievement, but merely getting over the same roadblocks and obstacles day after day leads down a path of minimized progress and maximized effort. Advancement comes from continual improvement.

First, update your schedule retroactively. This embodies the closure phase of project management. When you review your day, make sure everything you did that day is accounted for. For example, suppose the afternoon consisted of a one-hour meeting with a client, five phone calls returned while on the road, some time spent writing down ideas for your project over coffee at a coffee shop, and a chance meeting with a colleague in the elevator. It would be very tempting, once you get back to your desk, to just turn to the next item on the agenda and keep on going. But it's essential that a few minutes be put aside to enter those activities retroactively on your schedule, as well as to schedule any follow-ups for those activities. Get all the information in there even though the activities have already happened. Though this may seem like redundancy or a waste of time, in actual fact, you're doing three great things:

- You are following through on your completed actions, scheduling whatever is to happen next so that nothing falls through the cracks.
- You are keeping your project plan complete by recording your activities for billing and/or project history purposes.
- You are providing reference points for continual improvement by observing the true durations of activities, delays, and mistakes.

Second, unload your recorder. Throughout the day, every day, you will p with thoughts, ideas, and facts. Some of these may be great points of inspiration, others just reminders, such as "Remember to call Mary about next week's meeting." Short-term memory is no place to try and to keep good ideas—one or more of them will slip away before you have a chance to act on them. When you get into the habit of recording everything by carrying a small voice recorder or a pen and paper with you (or even calling your own voicemail), every idea gets committed to permanence. Then, during your I-Beam Base Review, you can unload all the great ideas and notes, and distribute them into your files and agenda as appropriate.

Is it really worth taking a minute and a half to enter details about a thirty-second phone call? Yes. The act of recording something commits it to searchable history. When you take time to log in activities, you're doing it for the future as well as for the past.

Third, analyze your activities in the name of continual improvement. There is a school of thought, a philosophy, actually, called *Kaizen*, best described by its founder, Masaaki Imai, as "continuing improvement in personal life, home life, social life, and working life."[1] The principles of continual improvement, like so many other areas of life, have to be revisited and practised if they are to become successful parts of your existence. A regularly scheduled I-Beam Base Review gives you the chance to do just this. For example, you might question:

- Why a meeting took so long: Are there ways to shorten and improve meetings?
- How much time did I spend traveling today? Could I have scheduled my activities to make better use of the day?
- Why did we encounter a crisis today? How could it have been avoided, and what steps should we implement to ensure it doesn't happen again?

Yikes, that sounds like extra work at the end of the day. But if you look at pro golfers, health care professionals, military generals,

---

1 Quoted from the homepage of the Kaizen Institute: www.kaizen-institute.com.

and many others you'll see that review and learning are part of the job. Why shouldn't you use the same opportunity? Rather than continuing to misuse time and energy in the future, a continual improvement review is your ticket to a more efficient way of working and greater success.

Fourth, add to your knowledge base. A knowledge base is your personal encyclopedia of facts, tips, and writings pulled from the resources around you and stored in an easy-to-use format. It is such a powerful tool for keeping yourself ahead of the pack in terms of industry knowledge and career-furthering intelligence that a complete how-to section is in Chapter 11. Maintaining your knowledge base daily by entering notes or quotes from information gathered throughout the day is akin to putting another dollar into a compound interest account. It may not seem worth it at the time, but its value increases with every passing day.

You can stop now. One additional benefit to scheduling and using the I-Beam Base is that it helps define the end of a day, and as such gives you permission to stop working. As we've seen, the constant influx and pace of work guarantee that the in-box will never be empty and the reactive nature of our central nervous system means the temptation to do "just one more thing" is always there. The I-Beam Base signals the end of the day and allows you to say, "I've done enough."

To summarize, the three parts of the I-Beam Agenda—the I-Beam Review, the middle, and the I-Beam Base—comprise a cohesive project plan for your workday. They work together to ensure you maximize control over every part of the day, while laying a path for improvement and advancement.

Your workday shouldn't start until the I-Beam Review has been completed, and shouldn't be considered over until the I-Beam Base has been dealt with. Sure, this means that fifteen minutes at the start and end of each day have to be put aside for planning. It means that you might have to fight the temptation to work or return a phone call during that time. It also means that your colleagues must accept that you are not to be disturbed even though you are physically there.

Later we will observe how the success components of a day—such as keystone time, payback time, opportunity time, prioritization skills, and the reserved blocks of predictable and unexpected activities—will best fit inside the I-Beam Agenda. But for that to happen, we'll need to know a little about how to sell the ideas to your colleagues and your boss. That's next ...

CHAPTER 5
INFLUENCE, CONDITIONING, AND COMMUNICATING

FLORENCE, ITALY, 1502

An enormous block of marble stood in the yard of the church of Santa Maria del Fiore. It had once been a magnificent piece of raw stone, but an unskilled sculptor had mistakenly bored a hole through it where there should have been a figure's legs, mutilating it. Florence's mayor, Piero Soderini, had contemplated trying to save the block by commissioning Leonardo da Vinci or some other master to work on it, but had given up, since everyone agreed that the stone had been ruined. So, despite the money that had been wasted on it, it gathered dust in the dark halls of the church.

This was where things stood until some Florentine friends of the great Michelangelo decided to write to the artist, then living in Rome. He alone, they said, could do something with the marble, which was still magnificent material.

Michelangelo traveled to Florence, examined the stone, and came to the conclusion that he could in fact carve a fine figure from it by adapting the pose to the way the rock had been mutilated. Soderini argued this was a waste of time—nobody could salvage such a disaster—but finally he agreed to let the artist work on it. Michelangelo decided he would depict a young David, sling in hand.

CHAPTER 5

Weeks later, as Michelangelo was putting the final touches on the statue, Soderini entered the studio. Fancying himself a bit of a connoisseur, he studied the huge work and told Michelangelo that while he thought it was magnificent, the nose, he judged, was too big.

Michelangelo realized Soderini was standing in a place right under the giant figure and did not have the proper perspective. Without a word, he gestured for Soderini to follow him up the scaffolding. Reaching the nose, he picked up his chisel, as well as a bit of marble dust that lay on the planks. With Soderini just a few feet below him on the scaffolding, Michelangelo started to tap gently with the chisel, letting the bits of dust he had gathered in his hand to fall little by little. He actually did nothing to change the nose, but gave every appearance of working on it. After a few minutes of this charade he called out: "Look at it now."

"I like it better," replied Soderini. "You've made it come alive."[1]

In this story, Michelangelo sought to change the mind of his boss not through confrontation, but by using his understanding of the mayor's ego to arrive at a satisfactory meeting of priorities. That's influence.

Influence is power, but it is not force. Influence helps people understand a new point of view by guiding their will in a new direction rather than battling it head-on.

Conditioning furthers the achievements gained from influence through positive reward. Many living creatures can be conditioned by way of a food reward after they perform a desired action. With human beings the same approach can be applied, but instead of food, we use another basic need, and that is comfort. A colleague, client, or manager needs comfort that his current need will be met. To address that need is to comfort. The approach you use to address that need will be recorded subconsciously by your colleagues in terms of future requests.

Communicating ensures that people receive the same "conditioning message" and get their heads around it. This can lead to "collective conditioning" when numerous members of your work community identify

---

1 Robert Greene, *The 48 Laws of Power* (New York: Viking, 1998), pp. 97–98, one of the best books ever written on the subject of human relationships.

the route to their comfort as being within the parameters of your new time management skills. (See, for example, "The Best Practices Meeting" (in Chapter 14) and Chapter 8: The Fifty-Five-Minute Meeting.)

To protect time and use it correctly, we must identify every opportunity to influence and soothe the wills and egos of those around us, and then ensure that people are compensated for playing along. Simply blocking off time or disappearing into an unused office to get work done, for example, runs the risk of causing the people around you to worry—not for your safety necessarily, but for the satisfaction of their own needs. Furthermore, choosing not to condition is still conditioning. Whichever response you give to a request or an interruption becomes a precedent for future expectations.

Let's put it this way: A colleague comes to you with a task that *he* perceives as urgent. He wants you to do it. If there is no one else who can do this task but you, then there are three possible answers you can give:

- I'll do it now.
- I'll do it later.
- I can't do it now, but I can do it at 2:00. How's 2:00 for you?

The first answer, "I'll do it now," informs the requestor that you are willing to drop everything to accommodate the request. That's not influence. Once precedent has been set, the expectation is that you will do so again and again, and you will lose control of that relationship. (And if you're thinking, "What if it's my boss who gives this request?" there are answers for that later in this chapter, under the heading "Huddles with Your Boss.")

The second answer, "I'll do it later," does not meet your colleague's need for comfort. He demands satisfaction, and a vague answer isn't enough. Any time we use avoidance without an acceptable alternative, the requestor remains motivated to pursue a better answer.

The third answer presents an acceptable alternative. In this case, 2:00p.m. is sufficiently close to soothe the requestor's need for satisfaction without requiring you to drop everything immediately. Providing that you actually deal with the request at 2:00p.m., you will have conditioned your colleague to recognize that you are accessible, albeit more on your own terms.

HOW TO GET THEM TO WANT TO DO WHAT YOU WANT THEM TO DO

Recently, IDEO, an avant-garde workplace design company, teamed up with "Dilbert" cartoonist Scott Adams to design the "ultimate cubicle." Of the many features of this design, one of the most intriguing was the "Murphy chair." Its premise was simple. Rather than having a second chair in the work area of a cubicle, the Murphy chair was actually a panel that would fold down from the cubicle wall to create a seating space, in much the same way a Murphy bed folds out of a wall to create a bedroom. From an influence perspective, the most fascinating aspect was that the Murphy chair was wired to the telephone in the cubicle, so that a few minutes after the seat was deployed, it made the phone ring, thereby prompting the visitor to realize that it was time to go. The seat-phone connection is a tool of influence, making or reminding a visitor of the need to leave due to a socially acceptable and higher-priority situation—"Oh, your phone's ringing. I should get going." For the reasons described in Chapter 1, technology appeals to an inner set of instinctive priorities and influences people to behave immediately.[2]

But when it's person-to-person, it's much more difficult to tell someone to go away and not interrupt your work, or to tell your boss that a project will take longer than she wants, or to inform someone that he is drifting off topic during a meeting. In any situation in which you must actively defend time, with no technology to lend credibility to your argument, you must pay careful attention to the words you use. They'll make all the difference.

The best strategy is to identify people's "comfort points" and factor those into your conversations. What can you say to let them know that you're defending time in *their* best interest? How can you explain it in such a way that they can see what you mean and share your vision? Many people refer to this as the "What's in it for me?" (WIIFM) factor. This is influence, but it requires you to take a moment to see the world from their perspective, to walk in their shoes.

---

2 Have a look at the IDEO's Ultimate Cubicle at www.ideo.com/dilbert/index.htm.

In later chapters you will see how to apply this to numerous situations in which you interact with colleagues and customers. But maybe it's best to start with the most important person of all: The boss.

HUDDLES WITH YOUR BOSS

Who is the person who has the most impact over your work activities? For most people, the answer would be their immediate superior, their manager, the senior partner—let's just call her the boss. Everyone works for someone. So, what will your boss think of your efforts to protect time through influence and conditioning?

As we've already seen, a central pillar of Cool Time is project management. The two words that define successful project management are "planning" and "communication." Project managers are taught that no matter how much pressure they are under, if they do not take time to plan, the project will fail. But the plan is not enough. They also learn that they must stay in constant communication with the people who are doing the work. They must share the vision of the project with them. They must inform, educate, and inspire. It's not enough to just say, "Do it."

How this applies to the relationship between you and your boss is illustrated in the importance of regular communication. Quite simply this means having "huddles"—daily if possible, or at least twice a week. It works in football, doesn't it? The team doesn't start a play without stopping to meet about it first, and with good reason. Even though all the players know how to play the game as it appeared at the start, it's essential to review and communicate constantly as the game unfolds.

A huddle is an essential part of influencing and conditioning your boss. Whether it happens daily or every couple of days, formally scheduled or on an *ad hoc* basis, how you do this depends on you, your boss, and the circumstances of your work. Whatever you decide, this huddle will be a chance to:

- review your schedule and your manager's schedule to make sure you each know what's planned for today, what should be done, and what can wait

- manage expectations—to inform each other at what stage each project is currently at, and how things are going
- actively listen—are there problems or issues that should be quickly addressed?
- prioritize together—are there conflicting tasks that need to be reviewed?
- plan for upcoming events—are there lead-in events or preparations for an upcoming trip or meeting that should be scheduled now?

Every opportunity you have for a huddle allows the boss to see clearly the tasks, time lines, and obstacles involved in the work she has assigned to you. Huddles are your chance to update her on a project or task and, in so doing, to influence her into accepting an alternate time line, one that satisfies her concerns about completion.

Putting out the ASAP fire. Think, for example, of the scenario in which a task or report is demanded ASAP, only to sit on the boss's desk for three days unread. One reason she asked for the report ASAP might be to protect herself from late delivery by artificially shortening the time line. If a previous request had gone ignored or forgotten, she would have learned to tighten up the time lines next time, and to trust no one.

You have an opportunity, by huddling regularly, to do three great things:

- First, nip this problem in the bud by learning more about the true date and circumstances surrounding this project.
- Second, demonstrate to her when, where, and how the project will be completed through the use of a clear project plan (your I-Beam Agenda).
- Third, recondition your boss by following through on the promise. Demonstrate through action that there is no longer a need to shorten time lines when it comes to you, since you will come through on time and keep her in the loop.

It may take weeks before she is willing to let go of the ASAP mentality. But your strategic huddle allows you to influence your boss by providing clear direction, suitable alternatives, and satisfaction of her priorities in a proactive and cool manner, rather than a reactive and stressed one.

The Gulf of Misperception. Your manager may have a different perception of what's involved in doing your job than you do. Even if she held that very same job before you took it on, things will have changed. She may have a misperception as to how long a task really takes or how necessary a piece of equipment (that you don't have) really is. She may even have a misperception of your productivity or reliability based on erroneous reports she has had from asking the wrong people at the wrong time. All of these situations and many more contribute to your manager's awareness of your workflow, which may or may not be accurate.

Having huddles might seem like a luxury, or it might seem that your boss or manager is not the kind of person who will be willing to undertake such a change in approach, but they are necessary to ensure that both of you remain on the same page and that there is no room for misunderstanding.

Sometimes the Onus Is on You

You may find, however, that success in influencing and conditioning the boss lies in taking care of some details in advance. For example, if she has a habit of flying off on a business trip and informing you only the day before, leaving you to drop everything to help her prepare, then perhaps it's best for you to insist on a regular meeting (huddle) to review her agenda for the longer term and prepare the needed materials well before the departure date. If your manager constantly shows up late for meetings, perhaps you could influence her schedule just a little to ensure that her prior appointment ends with enough time for her to arrive punctually. Is this extra work for you? Yes, but if it results in time saved and crises avoided elsewhere, then it becomes worth the effort. It will make her look good in the eyes of her peers and superiors, and strengthen the working relationship between the two of you, while keeping workload and time more under your control.

Managing the boss is called managing up, and it's essential to recognize that this is not an exercise in confrontation or in challenging the abilities or authority of the person to whom you report. It is instead an opportunity for ongoing communication and understanding, and is far more preferable than finding out all that is good and bad about your relationship at a once-a-year performance review.

One of the best books on managing up is called *Throwing the Elephant* by Stanley Bing. It delivers a lighthearted yet solid lesson on this essential professional skill by comparing the relationship you have with your boss to that between an elephant and its groomer. You are the groomer, and the boss is the elephant, entitled to sit wherever it wants and essentially do whatever it wants. Among the many points of this book is that although the elephant vastly outweighs you, you as the groomer would be wise to take the initiative, feeding and grooming the elephant before it knows it needs it. The last thing anyone needs is a ravenous angry elephant. Sometimes the best way to manage a symbiotic relationship such as that between you and your boss is to recognize it as such, and to take upon yourself the role of managing your manager for the good of your projects, your career, and your time.[3]

THE MAXED-OUT SCHEDULE

Many people suffering from overloaded agendas refer to the condition as having a maxed-out schedule. This is an interesting term, being so closely tied to credit cards, another aspect of our lives in which control is so easily lost. In the financial world, our credit rating represents financial credibility, a statement of trustworthiness that banks and others refer to in order to determine what type of risk each of us poses.

At work, people hold a similar assessment of us, primarily centered on their own instinctive comfort concerns. Their willingness to play ball with your Cool Time solutions, such as deflecting their requests to a later time, will be based on their credibility rating of you. No matter what you know or believe about yourself and your own reliability, each person around you must determine that for himself or herself. This is a rating that is built up over time, based on first impressions, then strengthened by actions and conditioning.

---

3 Stanley Bing, *Throwing the Elephant: Zen and the Art of Managing Up*, (HarperBusiness June 1, 2003).

Building and maintaining a strong credibility rating with colleagues, clients, and managers is easy. It's about positive payback—conditioning through reward. We will apply this to specific circumstances in the chapters that follow.

IS CONDITIONING REALLY POSSIBLE?

There's an old expression that says, "Choosing not to decide is still a decision," and as we established at the start of this chapter, the same applies in your relationships with your people: Choosing not to condition people is still conditioning. By starting meetings late (out of politeness or any other reason), by overloading your schedule (even with the best of intentions), and delivering tasks late or inaccurately, by working while under stress or out of control, you teach those around you what they can expect of you and what this means to their comfort instinct. This in turn builds their credibility rating of you, which influences how they will behave, and what they will expect of you in future situations.

PULLING TOGETHER INVENTORY AND INFLUENCE

Conditioning your colleagues and your boss is a skill that requires clear thinking and planning. Just as it takes money to make money, it takes cool to be Cool. When you feel stressed or conflicted, it becomes more difficult to remember the techniques needed to communicate alternate solutions to colleagues or to manage up with the boss.

That's where one of the great payoffs of inventory-based planning emerges. Once you have a sense of your schedule, once you have created a realistic work plan that takes into account the predictable and expectable actions of the day, once you know what you have on your plate and can demonstrate this to others, you liberate the short-term memory area of your brain, allowing it to focus on the immediate act of negotiation and influence. Without this tangible tool, your mind will be preoccupied with both sorting out the conflicting pressures in front of you and explaining them in vague, weak ways.

COMMUNICATION AND BRANDING

A HANDFUL OF WATER

The human body is roughly 70 percent water. In the temperature range in which humans are best suited to live, we experience water as a liquid, shapeless, yet powerful.

If you were to ask someone for a glass of water and he merely emptied a glassful over your head, you would probably be annoyed. Poured water is difficult to catch.

Yet when someone hands you a glass of water, it becomes eminently usable. You can carry the glass, pick it up, and put it down. The amorphous water is contained in a glass that you and everyone around you can see.

So it is with ideas and concepts. When they are presented verbally, with the intention of convincing others, they are vague and shapeless. Yet when they are contained within recognizable vessels that the other can touch and experience, they become real.

Real, practical agendas and plans with commonly understood names give the shapeless concept of busy-ness a tangible reality in the minds of those you seek to influence.

You can speed up the influencing and conditioning process by using Cool Time terminology when explaining your new best practices. Show your colleagues you're unavailable because you're in your keystone time, not simply because "you're kinda busy." Start to "brand" your private-focused work time as a combined keystone time/payback time and help them associate that term with "Do-not-disturb-unless-it's-really-important-and-remember-I'll-pay-you-back-in-half-an-hour." It's like the difference between free-flowing water and water inside a glass. One is intangible and hard to grasp ("I'm kinda busy right now"), the other is specific and clearly understandable ("My keystone time is scheduled for 10:00A.M. to 11:00A.M., and my payback time is from 11:00A.M. to 11:30A.M."). And if they don't know what keystone time is, explain it, including its benefits, using the printable explanation available on the cool-time.com website.

Use the other terms in this book as well: I-Beam Agenda, opportunity time, the fifty-five-minute meeting, and the sixty-second work space. They all have positive potential as tools of conditioning and influence. If you want, you can make up your own names for these things. The important thing is that you take advantage of the human need to use brands to make things familiar and comfortable. The next time you ask a colleague for a Kleenex or an Aspirin, ask yourself why you didn't instead request a paper tissue, or 200 mg of acetylsalicylic acid. You will be able to neatly package and deploy your time management strategies if you back them up with recognizable brands and then deliver them to your office community.

Next, let's look at some of those specific things that can be scheduled into your day to best handle your work inventory.

CHAPTER 6
APPLICATION: PRODUCTIVITY TECHNIQUES

KEYSTONE TIME

THE ROMAN ARCH

Back in the days when structures were built with stone, great respect was given to the arch as a system of supporting weight. Bridges, aqueducts, and windows were built using archways, and at the topmost point of the arch would be the keystone, a massive stone designed to absorb the pressures of the arch and the weight of the structure above it. The keystone was the central support. Without it the rest of the structure would be in danger of collapse.

Keystone time refers to a block of time in the day dedicated to almost (not completely) undisturbed work. It is one of the most useful techniques for getting things done, since work done during keystone time can be done much faster and better than when it is done between phone calls and other interruptions. If you let it, keystone time can be the support structure of your entire day.

Keystone time might be one hour in length, maybe two hours, maybe only half an hour. It depends on your line of work and your schedule. Within that time you work on the task that is most important to you—the top priority on your list—the task that has the highest payoff, the highest value, the number one priority identified in your I-Beam Review. This is your chance for pure productivity. Your keystone time doesn't have to be the same duration each day, nor does it have to be the same time each day, though it's advisable to try and make it coincide with your "best" metabolic time. But from a productivity standpoint, it's the highlight, the centerpiece.

Keystone Time: An Oasis of Focus

Firstly, keystone time works so well because the human brain enjoys focusing. In fact, multitasking, a term at the heart of many job descriptions, leads to unreal expectations about productivity. Your conscious brain operates in a manner similar to the computer you have on your desk. Even with its amazing speed and versatility, it processes conscious activities serially, so that you can pay attention to only one item at a time. Sure, you may have a dozen things on the go, but only one of them can be in focus at any given moment. Keystone time allows you that focus.

Secondly, when your mind becomes aware that there is only a fixed amount of time to get something done, it is more apt to deal with it efficiently than it would if you just planned to "work until it's finished." This is akin to running a race when you know the distance you're expected to run. When you give your body and mind clear parameters of when to start and end a task, it has a greater ability to consolidate, focus, and drive toward its goal. This focus on end times is a great motivator, and you'll see it play a major role not only in influencing people to leave you alone during keystone time (later in this chapter), but also to get them to show up on time for meetings (Chapter 8).

Thirdly, the human body does not function at a constant energy level throughout the day. It rises and falls, reaching peaks and valleys as the day wears on. Concentrating your energy into a smaller period within the day, especially at that time of the day when you are at your best, encourages greater achievement and productivity. According to the Pareto principle (Chapter 7), 80 percent of a day's achievement comes from 20 percent of the time available. Consider your keystone time to be the 20 percent of time that counts the most.

THE TRACTOR-TRAILER

Have you ever watched a tractor-trailer pull away from a stoplight? It doesn't exactly disappear in a cloud of dust. It lumbers away, shifting through its gears a few feet at a time. It takes the best part of half a mile before it's back up to cruising speed again. This analogy serves well to illustrate a problem that happens whenever we are interrupted at work. Imagine that stoplight as representing a single distraction in your day, such as the arrival of an e-mail or a drop-in visitor. We tend to think that as soon as the distraction is over, we can get back to what we were doing with little interruption. But, in fact, it takes much longer for the mind to regain the momentum it had before the interruption. Just like that large truck pulling away from the intersection, it can take five or ten minutes before you regain the same level of concentration that you enjoyed before the interruption. That period involves a shifting of gears, a slow mental refocus, a subconscious version of "Now let's see ... where was I?" When you think of the number of times you get distracted in any given day, it means that most of the day is spent trying to get back up to speed, and working at less than optimum productivity. Can you put a dollar figure on that?

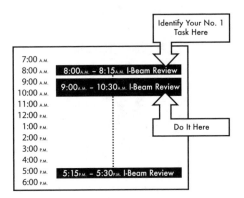

Figure 6.1: Keystone Time allows you to get your most important work done, as identified during your I-Beam Review.

The level of focus and concentration that is achievable during keystone time is not something that can be maintained for an entire day; it's a short-spell, high-impact, high-achievement device. It's a sprint, with a fixed duration and a clear finish line. It will help you feel terrific, since the satisfaction that comes from the knowledge that you have attained your day's goal, especially if you do so before lunch, provides a boost that drives you even further forward while helping to alleviate some of the day's stresses. Everything else you achieve after a keystone time feels like a bonus. It enables you to go home each night at a reasonable hour while your mind reflects upon the day's achievements, rather than fretting over unfinished business.

The Proof Is in the Pudding, as in "Pudding in" Extra Hours

Finding proof that keystone time works is easy. Look at how many people routinely stay late after the close of business hours to catch up on the day's work. Are you one of them? When asked why they do this night after night, they often answer, "Because that's when the phone stops ringing. I can finally get some work done." They have demonstrated the practical value of keystone time as a block of undisturbed focus time. Now it's time to make sure it happens during daylight hours.

The Price of Privacy: Payback

Most people would agree that a block of undisturbed time would be nice. Many time management books suggest it, but in the real world, locking yourself away for an hour is not an option. As we have already seen, humans operate on a level that speaks to the desire for comfort versus the fear of the unknown. Urgency supercedes all else. If your door is closed or you're otherwise unreachable, leaving no clues as to when you'll be back, that's an "unknown" in your colleague's book. The fear of that "unknown" will prompt her to seek instant connection with you by dropping in or calling.

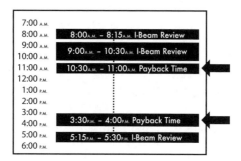

Figure 6.2: Keystone Time must be scheduled as two pieces: the first part for you, and the second part, Payback Time, for those who need to see you. Without the second part, the first part will fail.

So, the main building block toward establishing successful keystone time is to *factor in payback time and stick to it.* If you want an hour of keystone time, then reserve an hour and a half—one hour of keystone time plus a half-hour of payback time.

This ensures time for those who left you alone during the main hour of keystone time. That's when they can come back to see you. That's how to manage their fears and expectations. That's what you can use to influence their actions—not by telling them when keystone time starts but when and how it ends, with time guaranteed to be given over to their needs. Your visitors will be more inclined to respect your keystone time if they can see an acceptable alternate time in which their concerns and issues can be addressed.

Just how much time you'll need for keystone time and payback time is something you can determine and refine when you do your post-day review as part of your I-Beam Base. This is Kaizen, continual improvement.

Reserve your keystone time/payback time in advance. Think back to the discussion of inventory (Chapter 3) when you can make great progress in managing time and influencing others when the activities that you know will happen on a given day are reserved in advance. The same applies to your keystone time and payback time. Schedule them now, together for each day, as recurring activities.

Use a buddy system. If you feel that calls and other interruptions cannot be put off for the duration of an effective keystone time, find a colleague who is also interested. Make a deal with this person that you will cover her calls during her keystone time, while she covers yours during your keystone time. This has a five-fold payoff:

- You get your focused work done during your keystone time.
- She gets her focused work done during her keystone time.
- Your incoming calls are still dealt with by a qualified person.
- Her incoming calls are still dealt with by a qualified person.
- The two of you develop a heightened working relationship.

Allow for a sixty-second qualifier. We live in a real world with real issues. Not everyone will buy into the keystone time concept (though most will), and sometimes there are issues that are best dealt with immediately, even if they cause a minor distraction. If a colleague has a question that can be answered in less than sixty seconds, then it's best to let him do it, providing that he sticks to that sixty-second rule. If he needs to know the location of a file or needs a signature from you, then give him what he needs. If he wants to talk about weightier issues, then remind him of the upcoming payback time. Remember the Hoover Dam story in Chapter 3—strength comes from flexibility. Payback time is like the dam's diversion channels—they alleviate stress by providing alternatives for the smaller pressures. Even though a sixty-second question is a distraction, it will still increase your focus time overall.

COMPONENTS OF A HIGH-IMPACT KEYSTONE TIME

Work in short blocks. The human mind does love to focus, but it needs to practice. Also, focus can be quite tiring—it takes a lot of energy to stay single-minded. In the physical world, if you stay in one position too long, one or more parts of your body will start to go numb, since muscles and bones need constant movement. The same applies to the brain. Attempting to stay focused for extended periods will result in brain numbness, usually in the form of frustration, distraction, an inability to concentrate, or the desire to sleep at one's desk.

Keep keystone times to one hour or ninety minutes at most. And throughout the day, not just during keystone time, give yourself a two-minute break every sixty minutes—time enough to stand up, look around, allow your eyes to change their focus, stretch. Do a few chair-based stretches, including reaching toward the ceiling and extending your arms fully outwards to stretch the rib cage and the upper back.[1]

Gather all the things you'll need and eliminate those you don't. Ensure all your files, notes, and other materials are available and within your line of sight. Remove from your field of view any documents, memos, or items that refer to other projects. Turn off the ringer on your phone, and close down your e-mail software, if possible. Your objective is to have all that you need and none of what you don't need within your field of view.

Get comfortable. Kick off your shoes. Make sure your chair is the right height and that your spine and feet are properly supported. Get your computer monitor, keyboard, and mouse aligned to your fore-arms, wrist, and line of sight. Get your refreshments lined up, and if you drink coffee or tea, balance them with water.

Build a cone of concentration. It is not yet possible to have a "cone of silence," an actual zone in the middle of a busy work area in which all sound is completely deadened, but you can do the next best thing by investing in a set of noise-reduction headphones (approximately $200) and some learning-focused music. Noise-reduction headphones

---

1 Some low-strain, no-sweat office exercises are available at the Cool-Time website at www.cool-time.com.

muffle much of the ambient noise in a general work environment (they are also excellent for reducing fatigue during air travel). They will not cut out voices, but they give a sense that everything is much farther away. The learning-focused music helps cut out ambient vocal noise simply by masking it with nonintrusive, pleasing sound. Learning-focused music is recommended in place of popular music, since it provides pleasing sound without recognizable works or melodies that can distract. An added benefit of using headphones is their use as props. People are less inclined to interrupt colleagues who are wearing headphones, especially when their keystone time sign lets them know when the headphones will be coming off.[2]

OF ALL THE GIN JOINTS IN ALL THE WORLD ...

Julius Epstein, along with his twin brother, Philip, wrote and revised some of the most famous screenplays in Hollywood history, including *Casablanca*. In the 1940s a temporary illness forced Jack Warner's studio to give Mr. Epstein permission to work from home on the screenplay, which he did. As a result, he was able to complete the work in half the time. He worked full out for two hours a day. Any more than that, he said, just resulted in inferior quality. The rest of the time, he played tennis or golf. Okay, so we don't all have tennis courts in our backyards, but doesn't it help to prove a point? Two hours of focus is better than ten hours of blur.

By the way, if you have reservations about how to introduce keystone time, payback time, and its sixty-second qualifier into your community, we will cover techniques for introduction and acceptance as part of implementation in Chapter 14.

---

2 Some suggested brands of both headphones and music are available at the Cool-Time website at www.cool-time.com.

OPPORTUNITY TIME

Many people who have succeeded in business and at work employ another tool that can be easily scheduled, defended, and explained, one that ensures they always have some time left for unexpected opportunity. Quite literally, opportunity time is an hour or so reserved for whatever will further their business.

There are many successful, high-profile people who can serve as role models for this—executives who have realized the importance of adding tactical opportunity time into their agendas. In her book *The Secret Handshake*, Kathleen Kelley Reardon profiles some very big names, like Jeff Bezos of Amazon.com, who "takes time to step back, set aside a fraction of time for his own, and … uses Tuesdays and Thursdays to reflect a bit and to say thank-you to people." Bezos has recognized that "not giving yourself some downtime is a sure way to lose sight of the objectives."[3]

Opportunity time is difficult to accept, since it goes against the existing conditioning of the North American work ethic, the one that says the only good agenda is a full agenda, and that achievement is best gained through unrelenting busy-ness. But really, opportunity time is simply an extension of the inventory exercise. Whereas the inventory in Chapter 3 accounted for predictable and expectable activities, opportunity time accounts for the truly unanticipated. Whether the unanticipated activity is a good one, such as a new client or an occasion to further develop your business/career, or a bad one such as a never-before-experienced crisis, if the situation presents itself, it is far easier to answer the call if you have time available for it.

We have a fixed amount of time per day available for use. When you book that time solid, embracing the critical path, that's like filling a bucket to the brim. When an opportunity or crisis happens, the additional work will result in overflow. Something's gotta give.

Thus, the goal is to keep 15 percent of the day's volume "unspoken for" and well defended, so you will be best prepared to handle the truly

---

3 Kathleen Kelley Reardon, Ph.D., *The Secred Handshake: Mastering the Politics of the Business Inner Circle* (New York: Doubleday, 2002) p.58.

unanticipated. Just as a paramedic would not assess a patient and then rush off to the pharmacy to buy the necessary supplies, neither should you try to find time only after you discover you need it. Having time or supplies available in advance allows them to be used in the best possible way.

Obviously, scheduling opportunity time can't be done overnight. It needs steady introduction and nurturing, practice, and review. Start small. Use the power of the reserved activity (Chapter 3) to insert just half an hour of opportunity time into each workday in next month's calendar, and the month after that, and beyond. Just half an hour. Use it when needed, and increase it as necessary.

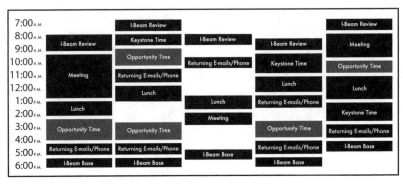

Figure 6.3: This image shows a sample week, in which of the various techniques discussed above have been inserted as recurring events. Remember, the motivation behind this is not to add more to your schedule, but to get the right priorities in the right order.

Opportunity time isn't about giving up 15 percent your day. It's about maximizing the productivity of the full 100 percent. And that feels great!

THE GOLDEN HOUR

In the movie business, there is a certain time of day—sometimes called the golden hour (actually only a precious few minutes)—during a sunset when the light is golden, warm, and clear. It is used for romantic shots, close-ups, and any situation where the actors and the story need to be bathed in visual warmth. The golden hour doesn't last very long, and there is seldom an opportunity for a second take within the same day. Once the sun is down, it's down. The crew has to work fast to get this most important shot done before the light fades.

There is a golden hour in the workday, and it, too, is very precious, unique, and not actually an hour in length—more like thirty minutes. As we established in Chapter 2, humans are a light-loving species. Our circadian rhythms, combined with the stimulus of early morning light, the energy of the travel into work, and the influence of food energy and caffeine, mean that for most people the period of highest alertness and energy is during the first thirty minutes of the day, roughly from 9:00a.m. to 9:30a.m. That's it. It's downhill from there.

This is important to remember as you use your I-Beam Agenda to plan your day. What will you do with those first thirty minutes? Use them to work at your peak of productivity by starting your keystone time then? Or should you schedule your meetings for the golden hour when almost everyone's energy levels would be reasonably high? How about planning your presentations in that time to ensure your audience stays alert? Or your huddles to get the most attention from a time-conscious manager?

To work better with your colleagues, it helps to understand the effect of circadian rhythms in pinpointing optimum times for meetings, presentations, and other gatherings. Though you can never please all people all of the time, your decision about when to schedule your next major strategy meeting should be more than simply one of agenda-matching or finding out when the board-room is free. Consciously aiming for that period in the day when most people are at their best, and consciously avoiding the time when they're guaranteed to be at their worst, ensures more successful meetings and more productive outcomes. Those three best times (for most people) are:

- 9:00a.m. to 10:00a.m. (the golden hour); followed by
- 10:45a.m. to 11:30a.m. (assuming they've had a mid-morning break and a snack)
- 1:00p.m. to 2:00p.m. (assuming they've had a lunch break)

Here is your opportunity to put some of these great principles to work for the benefit of the entire department and, of course, for you.

- First, schedule your most important meetings for the golden hour.
- Next, use the techniques of running truly effective meetings (Chapter 8) to ensure the meeting pays off, not only in terms of creativity, but also by satisfying all participants as to its relevance and value.
- Finally, use part of your I-Beam Base to review the meeting, to apply continual improvement questions to identify how well the meeting went, where the problems were, and how the meeting could be improved for next time. Remember, when you are interacting with people, such as in a meeting, you are conditioning them. Whether the meeting experience is good or bad, the people around the table are being conditioned to react accordingly, and always in their own interests—that's human nature. Bad, uncomfortable meetings condition them to stay away, avoid, or disrupt the event. Great meetings condition them to want to attend, participate, and contribute. By keeping this in mind during the *Kaizen* portion of the I-Beam Base, you extract the very best of the people around you in the shortest possible time period. That's the power of the golden hour.

CARRYOVER MOMENTUM

The power of a little planning is an amazing thing. Whatever day of the week it is as you read these lines, think back to what you were doing one week ago. Doesn't seem like seven days, does it? It's not fair how quickly time seems to fly, but that's life.

If you are faced with a task that is too big to get done all at once, the chances are that another week will slip by, then another, then another. Though this might be considered procrastination, it's not always the case that you're actually consciously putting it off, so much as never quite getting around to it—there's a difference.

To that end, there is the principle of carryover momentum, in which we can break up a large task, schedule and deal with it regularly and consistently over a period of days.

If you were to assign one hour per day to a project, you wouldn't feel that you were making any headway after the first hour on the first day. But if you were able work on the project one hour each workday for a month, that would be twenty hours, or two-and-a-half full business days. For larger-scale projects, that one hour per day, even with weekends and holidays off, would become 250 hours in a year, or the equivalent of one month's worth of workdays. That's a lot of time!

The reason why this technique is called carryover momentum goes back once again to the workings of the brain. By returning to an ongoing task on a daily basis—preferably, but not necessarily at the same time each day—the mind continues to retain and access the creative momentum of the previous day. It significantly reduces the amount of "Let's see now, where was I?" that happens when work on a project is resumed after a week or two of inactivity.

This is yet another example of how to capitalize on the strengths and weaknesses of the brain to get the right work done in the right way within the constraints of a busy day.

Here is where we are so far. We've looked at a number of the features that go into how a day can be structured, using inventory as our primary tool. Next, we need to look at the motivations and concerns of the people you work with, as well as your own motivations, to see how these ideas can be effectively communicated and accepted.

CHAPTER 7
PRODUCTIVITY: HOW DO YOU KNOW IF YOU'RE BEING PRODUCTIVE?

THE PARETO PRINCIPLE

In 1906, an Italian economist, Vilfredo Pareto observed that 20 percent of the Italian people owned 80 percent of his country's accumulated wealth.[1] It was the official start of a famous rule now known as the Pareto principle, or the 80/20 rule. It is a versatile principle that helps describe the many areas of human activity in which a small amount of something has great impact over a larger amount.

When taking inventory of plans, situations, and goals, the 80/20 rule helps both to identify activities that have the greatest value, and to remind us that success comes more easily when allowances are made.

For example, it can be said that 80 percent of our productivity and achievement comes from 20 percent of our day. It seems we work hard all day, every day, that we are always busy, that there never seems to be enough time. But in truth, the ratio of real productivity to perceived work is a surprising one.

1 Arthur W. Hafner, Ph.D., M.B.A, *Pareto's Principle: The 80-20 Rule*, Seton Hall University, http://library.shu.edu

If you've gone on a diet, for example, you've probably been told to rigorously track every piece of food that passes your lips. Either by assigning a point value to each bite, or by logging it into a record book, nutritionists emphasize the importance of honestly recording every piece of food that we eat. Why? Because what we think we eat and what we actually eat are very different. Serving sizes, snacks, little things here and there add up to much more than we care to admit. The same thing happens during the workday. The activities and distractions that go unnoticed or accepted as day-to-day work add up to a surprising amount of lost time.

EXTERNAL TIME EATERS

Let's refer to our inventory technique to look at some of the many things that keep us from getting our real work done. These are predictable distractions that come at us from every direction, every day, and they don't just pull us away from the work at hand, they also make us forget the constant passage of time. They have been accepted and absorbed as a normal part of our workplace existence.

External time eaters (as opposed to internal time eaters described next) are products of our working environment. They are external events that capture our attention and rob us of our control of the moment. They include:

- delays leaving the house (can't find my keys!)
- commuting delays
- conversations/small talk with colleagues
- computer and network problems
- dealing with e-mail
- attending meetings
- looking for things
- taking and making phone calls
- attending training sessions
- receiving visitors
- listening to voicemail

INTERNAL TIME EATERS

There are also time inefficiencies whose origins are internal. These are personality-driven traits or actions that cause delay, pressure, and stress. They are often more difficult to spot than external time eaters because they are part of our own personal makeup. They include:

- not saying no to additional tasks
- reluctance to delegate
- attempting too much at once
- becoming immune to static to-do lists
- ineffective prioritization skills
- starting before all facts/tools are available
- setting unrealistic estimates
- not setting deadlines at all
- wanting to always appear available
- not keeping track of the progress of tasks
- procrastinating
- getting distracted
- accommodating interruptions
- not listening or not hearing
- not taking notes
- socializing a little too much
- working without adequate rest
- relying on a system that is all in your head

As difficult as they are to spot, internal time eaters are also more difficult to eliminate since they are part of our own personality. So much of what we do is simply done according to internal social motivations: If someone is chatting with you in your office, it's considered rude to bring the conversation to a halt, so we wait. These actions are not factored into our perception of the time available for work in any given day. Few people will stop to calculate how long it takes to refill the coffee machine or fix a copier jam, but those minutes are being spent, not loaned. Our actions inspired by internal motivation come back to haunt us when day turns to night and we find ourselves still at the office.

Can we eliminate all these external and internal time eaters? Should we? Well, not all of them.[2] The idea is to be aware of their existence and to be cautious about the surprising level of influence they have. We cannot defeat an enemy until we understand it, and recognizing the sheer amount of time in a workday that is devoured by external and internal time eaters opens the door to the potential of increased achievement within the same number of hours.

REALISTIC TIME ASSESSMENTS FROM THE WORLD OF PROJECT MANAGEMENT

So what do internal and external time eaters have to do with the Pareto principle and productivity? For a start, they help answer the question "Where does the time go?" They show that the amount of time left over for the real productive work of the day is surprisingly small—so small that it's almost insulting.

Remember in Chapter 2 when we talked about taking a stopwatch to a football game, and how that correlates to the workplace? And remember how we discussed how project management plays such a major role in successful time management? A project manager understands that for every person-day available to spend on a project, he must allow for between two and three hours of productive time per day, not the eight or ten you'd expect. Only a small fraction of the day is given over to true productivity. The rest of the time is spent in support activities. Simply put, 20 percent of your day—Pareto's magic number—is the really good stuff.

But which 20 percent? This is a matter for you to identify by focusing on clues such as your personal energy levels, the busy-ness of your workplace, the frequency of interruptions and crises, your ability to focus, your ability to handle deadlines and pressure, and, of course, your inventory. This is precisely the type of discovery that is afforded by the I-Beam Base—the *Kaizen* portion—as you end and review your day.

---

2 Remedies for all of the issues described above are available in this book. Consult the Quick Reference list next to the Table of Contents.

You might have a job where optimum time for keystone time/ payback time is obvious, perhaps between 4:00 p.m. and 5:30 p.m. after the phones stop ringing, the markets have closed, or as most of your colleagues head home. Perhaps the morning is better. Some people schedule keystone time for the lunch hour when there are fewer colleagues around, which is a great strategy, provided you allow some time to eat just prior to or just after this productive block.

But for many others, keystone time is something that must be scheduled and defended. This takes practice and perseverance. But once you become adept at focusing in on this crucial 20 percent of your day, you will be able to double your productivity.

OTHER PARETO APPLICATIONS

Twenty percent of your incoming calls will yield 80 percent of your business. During the course of the day you will receive many calls and e-mails, but they are not all of the same importance. During keystone time, for example, if a high-priority client calls, of course it makes sense to take that call. It's worth it. But the others can wait. They're not urgent; they just seem that way. And as long as your substantive voicemail greeting manages the expectations of those callers (see Chapter 10), you can focus on what you need to focus on. Ignore 80 percent of your interruptions and allow the other 20 percent in. That's far more productive than accepting everything and never getting around to the important work.

Twenty percent of your colleagues aren't going to play ball with this. Some will still interrupt, distract, and lay waste to your time management plans. Some people just have that kind of personality. Also, your boss and other high-ranking people will also have a different set of privileges, though most managers will be surprisingly accepting of Cool Time initiatives once they're educated about them. (See "Huddles with Your Boss," page 57.) If you can eliminate 80 percent of walk-in interruptions, you will still win overall.

Eighty percent of a meeting's productivity comes from 20 percent of its duration. Just like the rest of the day, a meeting is an event that is rife with time wasters. We cover this fully in Chapter 8.

Fill your day calendar 80 percent full and leave 20 percent empty. This is covered as "Opportunity Time" in Chapter 6.

All of this Cool Time stuff will work only 80 percent of the time. There are some phone calls and people that should be seen to right away. Some meetings will still go overtime, there will still be crunches and crises, and there will always be some things beyond your control. The trick is to aim to reduce 80 percent of the time-related problems in your life. If you aim to eliminate 100 percent, the odds are that something will slip through, which might disappoint you. Aim for excellence rather than perfection.

PRIORITIZING AND TRIAGE

Probably the most common question asked at time management workshops is, "How do I prioritize all the tasks that I have to get done?" Much like the "magic-bullet aerosol spray" described in Chapter 1, people are looking for the formula to help them deal with the mental chaos that comes from conflicting tasks.

Let's look first at a situation that is probably far more life-and-death-like than any of us will hopefully ever have to face, and that's emergency triage. The traditional battlefield definition, credited to a surgeon in Napoleon's army, refers to the technique of sorting out a group of injured people into three categories (from the French word *trier*, "to sort") so that the most serious cases are treated first or by the appropriate specialist. The three categories are: (1) those who will survive if given immediate medical help; (2) those who will survive with medical help, but can wait a little while; and (3) those who won't survive. It's an act of Cool judgment in the most extreme situations, such as on the battlefield, at accident scenes, and in the emergency room. The obvious message here is that medical professionals, whom we come to rely on to solve life-or-death situations, rarely lose their cool. Though they cannot predict what emergency or crisis will be next, they will always take a few moments to sort out priorities using objective procedure rather than subjective, emotion-based decisions before they begin.

Translating battlefield triage to your personal agenda requires the same cool head and the same ability to sort out the critical from the mundane. It also requires that you recognize from the outset that there is only one of you, and you can do only one thing at a time.

Take, for example, the term "multitasking." This horrible term has mutated within the collective unconscious from its original meaning of "being able to do a number of tasks" to "being able to do a number of tasks simultaneously." This is akin to choosing a bucket rather than a hosepipe to extinguish a fire. When water is thrown from a bucket, the water is distributed randomly and ineffectively, much of it missing its target. If the same amount of water is pumped from a bucket through a hose, the jet can be concentrated at the base of the flames for better results.

Prioritization is triage. The best plan of action is in ensuring that work is viewed not by a false sense of immediate urgency, but through the filters of cool, higher-level assessment.

First, turn to gut feeling. Most of us have a sense of which task should be dealt with first, based on current knowledge of things going on in the business and in the office. Whether you're setting up your day during your I-Beam Review or whether a colleague drops another project on your desk while you're hard at work at something else, make sure stress doesn't overtake the Cool thinking of triage. Don't get caught up in the false urgency that your central nervous system thinks it's seeing. Not everything in front of you should be dealt with first. The best prioritization technique is to allow yourself the time to stop, think, and then plan.

Recall from Chapter 3 that the more you craft and refine your inventory, the more time you will be able to reserve in advance for the types of work that you can reasonably predict and expect on a given day.

Second, place each task in the perspective of urgency and importance. One of the greatest lessons from Stephen Covey's classic *The 7 Habits of Highly Effective People* is to ensure that tasks fulfill the criteria of being both highest in urgency (usually deadline related), and also highest in importance (contributing to your main mission).[3]

If the tasks confronting you still seem to be equal and conflicting, it's time for some interrogation. You might want to assess the tasks according to this checklist to see which one emerges as number one:

---

3 Stephen Covey, *The 7 Habits of Highly Effective People*, New York, Fireside (Simon & Schuster), 1989.

- Is this task directly related to one of my top three current projects?
- Does this task need to be completed today?
- Does this task need to be done by me or should it be delegated?
- Does this task have high value to my manager or client that he will notice if it is not done?
- Can this task be quickly taken care of?
- If I don't do this task immediately, will the resulting trouble be greater than the gains I expect to achieve from it?
- If I have to put aside something else to do this task, will the benefit be greater than the task I'm currently doing?
- What if I don't do this task at all?
- What will this task mean to me a week from now?
- What will this task mean to me a year from now?
- Is this task directly related to my job's responsibilities or are there job-related tasks I should put before it?

These questions neutralize the urgency of change by placing the new task in proper perspective, in other words, triage. For example, the final question sounds like people should merely "work to rule," but that's not the case. If your job is in accounting, let's say, and someone comes to you with a computer-related problem, and you take it on just because you happen to know how to fix the problem or because no one else is around to help out at that moment, then you set yourself up for two main problems:

- First, you place a task that is unrelated to your work before your own priorities.
- Second, you set a precedent, conditioning the requestor to come back to you for the same type of assistance the next time it happens. This should be nipped in the bud early by saying something such as "I'm doing this once for you as a special favor, but in future, you should talk to Mary about these types of problems."

This is why "Huddles with Your Boss" (Chapter 5) are so important. Only through regular and frequent communication can you, your colleagues, and your manager work together to ensure that your time is being used best: on the work you're best suited for and for which you are primarily accountable.

WHEN THERE'S NO TIME FOR PRIORITIZING: KEEPING COOL IN A CRISIS

THE STORY OF CHUKO LIANG

On the eve of an important river battle, the great third-century Chinese strategist Chuko Liang found himself falsely accused of secretly working for the other side. As proof of his loyalty, his commander ordered him to produce 100,000 arrows for the army within three days or be put to death. Instead of trying to manufacture the arrows, an impossible task, Liang took a dozen boats and had bundles of straw lashed to their sides. In the late afternoon, when mist always blanketed the river, he floated the boats toward the enemy camp. Fearing a trap from the wily Chuko Liang, the enemy did not attack the barely visible boats with boats of their own, but showered them with arrows from the bank. As Liang's boats inched closer, they redoubled the rain of arrows, which stuck in the thick straw. After several hours, the men hiding on board sailed the vessels quickly downstream where Chuko Liang met them and collected his 100,000 arrows.[4]

The Chuko Liang story illustrates the beauty of grace under pressure—of keeping a cool head. Today, we use the term "firefighting" in the context of business situations to describe the art of quickly resolving a crisis.

There are some who pride themselves on being masters at putting out such "fires," and if they truly are good at it, it's because they know how to remain in control. For most of us, however, firefighting is

---

4 Robert Greene, *The 48 Laws of Power* (New York: Viking, 1998), pp. 211–212.

not comfortable. It requires that we focus resources and energies on a situation that should never have been allowed to happen. It diverts us from the real priorities of the day, priorities that will now have to be put off, which in turn compounds the existing workload and builds a mountain of unstarted and unfinished work. Fighting fires also means using instant, hurried judgment; risking irrational, improper decisions; and less-than-productive outcomes.

If you are in the midst of a crisis at this moment, remember there are rules to follow:

Be aware of overreaction. Crises do have solutions. They may require urgent phone calls, changes of plans, fast travel, and fast thinking, but crises can be resolved. What is crucial during a crisis is clear thinking and the avoidance of "alarm mindset." Don't fall prey to your first instinct. Take a moment to assess the situation and plan the most expedient and practical course of events to solve it.

Never succumb to anger. Anger makes people do irrational and possibly long-remembered, negative things. Anger is the ultimate example of stress pushing aside the rational part of the brain. During periods of anger and frustration, the best thing to do is to breathe deeply, and count to ten—seriously. Few things done in anger can ever be repaired entirely. Often, the damage that anger causes lasts longer than the crisis itself. Ask yourself if it will really matter a year from now. And, if so, in what way?

Avoid angering/panicking others. Panic and anger are contagious. When one person displays these emotions, it becomes very easy for them to affect everyone else. But similarly, so does calm. A calming presence in the face of fear can just as easily be picked up by those around you. When you take the time to pull your own "cool" back together, you stand a great chance of inspiring others to do the same.

Avoid the superhero syndrome. This is the feeling that everything must be done by you and you alone. This is commonly felt by people who are used to decision making and fast action. However, more can be done through delegation and leadership than by becoming a single-person rescue squad. Take the time to assess your resources, assign tasks appropriately, and follow up with them to ensure that nothing gets left behind. (More on the superhero syndrome in Chapter 15.)

Use checklists. If you have prepared a crisis checklist, be sure to use it. Make sure you know where it is. Make sure other people know where it is and how to use it, as the odds are always greatest that the person who best knows what to do in a particular crisis will be on vacation when it happens.

Ask yourself, "What would happen if I did nothing?" Some crises can be left to blow themselves out. Urgency and adrenaline sometimes make us do more than is actually necessary. Assess the nature of the crisis and consider whether your actions would solve or prolong the situation.

THE OVERBOARD RULE

Here's a classic example of how both keeping a cool head and avoiding the superhero syndrome pay off out on the water. If you're on a boat and you see someone fall into the water, your responsibility from the moment you shout "Man overboard!" is to never take your eyes off the person and keep pointing to where he is. You let someone else bring the boat around, and someone else prepare the rescue. If you were to lose sight of the person, especially in choppy waters, you might not be able to locate him again. Teamwork, a cool head, and adherence to existing crisis management rules stand a far greater chance of saving a life.

No fire should ever have to be fought twice. Once an unexpected crisis has been resolved, it now becomes part of your collective knowledge, an experience that can be planned for in the future. In your post-crisis meeting you ask (and answer):

- What happened to precipitate this crisis?
- How did we fix it?
- How well did we fix it?

- What can we do to prevent this from happening again? Or:
- What are the odds of it happening again, and how will we prepare for it next time?

WHAT A FIASCO!

Fiasco is a term used to describe a mess, a screw-up, the kind of thing you don't want to happen again.

It comes from the Italian word for "bottle." When the glassblowers of medieval Italy made a mistake and their beautiful, delicate glass sculpture collapsed while being blown, all they could do to cut their losses was to reshape the glass and sell their ruined work as a bottle, a *fiasco*.

OTHER PRIORITIZATION TECHNIQUES

If you recognize that the conflicting tasks in front of you share the same levels of urgency and importance, have passed the triage test above, and still need to be done by you right now, then do the following.

Get the small tasks out of the way first. If small tasks are obscuring your view of a larger, more important task, then clear your mind of these "hangers-on" by doing them first. Use your I-Beam Review to list the tasks, along with their expected durations, directly into your day's agenda. Always bear in mind the importance of making this list tangible on paper or on screen, not just in your head.

Alternately, do the larger task first. If your mindset is one that prefers to get big things out of the way first, then do the big thing, and then enjoy the feeling of achievement that it brings.

Delegate upward. Most people think of delegation as passing work to someone else, but upward delegation can also refer to involving your manager/client in the decision-making process. If you have two or more tasks that appear to have equal validity, importance, and urgency, and you can't decide which one should be done first, and if there is a risk of negative repercussions if one of the tasks doesn't get done, then it is safer and more proactive on your part to involve the stakeholder. Similarly, if you work for two or more people, each of whom thinks her tasks are the more important, you risk being caught in a power squeeze in which you'll come out the loser. Conflicting priorities between two managers need to be recognized and resolved between the three of you.

Inviting your manager(s) to assist you in the triage process is not complaining. It's a proactive meeting of minds intended to get the right work done in the right way. A quick huddle that lets all sides know what you're working on and what you're not and ensures that expectations are suitably managed.

THE SMARTS TEST

This is a technique for prioritization taken straight from the pages of project management. It helps assess whether the task before you can and should be done by you, or whether more information is needed. Should you find yourself faced with a vague project or task that you can't get a handle on, it's worth reviewing this procedure before moving ahead. It's also strong background material for consulting (upward delegation) with your manager. SMARTS is an acronym that stands for the following:

Specific: Is the task definite? Is it an identifiable task, or is it a vague collection of subtasks? "Buy a loaf of brown bread" is a specific task. "Ensure the pantry is stocked" is not specific.

Measurable: Can you measure the task? How can you tell when the task is complete? When does it start? When does it end? "Redesign the company website" is not a measurable task—it's too vague. Does the website project end when the site goes live? What about ongoing maintenance, updates, and corrections? Is that part of the project, or is it a separate project? What clearly defines the parameters of this task?

Achievable: Can this task be done? Is it possible? If you ask me to install a marble tile floor in your foyer and I have no experience or skill in this area, then the task is not achievable, no matter how much money or time you offer me.

Realistic: Using the marble floor example above, assume that I am qualified to do the work. If the job takes two days to do, and I have nothing else scheduled for the next two days, then, yes, I can do it, and it would be realistic to estimate and quote the job as a two-day job. However, if my schedule is full, and I can't even get to your house before the end of next week, then promising two-day delivery is not realistic, even though I'm qualified to do the work.

Time-oriented: Is there a schedule, a time line, a deadline for the completion of the task? This ties in closely with the "measurable" principle, in that I'll need to know not only what defines the start and end of a project, but also the dates for starting, ending, reviewing, delivery, etc. Without written time lines, it's easy for a task to drift or to move onto the critical path.

Signed-off: To whom do I report? Who is the person who approves this project, who will be authorized to accept the finished product, and to whom all questions and issues should be directed? Who am I working for on this project?

The SMARTS test ensures that before any actual work is done, there is a clear understanding of the scope and the parameters involved. It's an example of stepping back and getting a higher-level view before proceeding.

DO THE RIGHT THING

In addition, when prioritizing all the tasks in front of you, remember that not all of them can get done. We routinely pack our days full of tasks of varying importance and payoff, and expect to get it all cleared by the end of the day, just so we can start again tomorrow. According to the 80/20 rule, 20 percent of the work we do yields 80 percent of the payoff. The rest is small stuff or stuff that has a misleading amount of urgency. It makes sense to identify, isolate, and focus on those activities that really pay off. Get them identified, scheduled in, with enough time to complete them rather than leaving them mixed in with the less valuable tasks. Your energy is finite, and your excellence should be treasured. Effort wasted in multitasking and working on insignificant tasks is lost forever. Identify the right thing and do it first and singularly. Remember the words of Confucius: "He who chases two rabbits catches none."

CHAPTER 8
THE FIFTY-FIVE-MINUTE MEETING: CONDITIONING IN THE BOARDROOM

THE NEVER-ENDING MEETING

In their classic book *How to Make Meetings Work,* authors Michael Doyle and David Straus first estimated that across America in 1976, there were 11 million meetings happening every business day. A recent update to that estimate puts the new number at 25 million per day.[1] If you were to accept the average meeting as lasting an hour and a half, with five people in attendance, that's 187,500,000 person-hours per day.

It's no surprise, then, that many consider meetings to be the single biggest time waster in the workday. Why? The usual suspects include the following:

1 Sauer, Patrick J. "Escape from Meeting Hell" *INC. Magazine* (May 2004), p. 70.

- There are too many of them.
- They don't start on time.
- They have unclear agendas.
- They go on for too long.
- The wrong people are invited.
- People introduce irrelevant topics.
- People "tune out" and do other work on their PDAs.
- They conclude with vague ideas and unresolved issues.
- They end late.

Meetings are intended to coordinate action, to exchange information; to motivate a team; discuss issues, ideas, or problems; and/or to make a decision. Do meetings always achieve these goals? Sometimes. Do they achieve them in the shortest time possible? Not often.

As mentioned in Chapter 7, according to the Pareto principle, 80 percent of the decisions and productivity of meetings comes from 20 percent of the meeting's duration.[2] It can be argued that you can get to those critical decisions only after having spent time brainstorming, talking, learning, and resolving conflicts, but most would agree that much of the time spent in meetings could be put to better use.

Meetings are a necessary part of business life, and the Cool Time approach seeks to make them more efficient and shorter by focusing once again on the motivations and concerns of the people involved, rather than on the meeting's topic. It is vital that we influence and condition them positively, to help them become active, punctual participants.

DURATION: FIFTY-FIVE MINUTES

First, never go longer than fifty-five minutes. Ergonomists will tell you it's unwise to keep people seated for more than an hour without a break, but that's not why the fifty-five-minute meeting is so successful.

It's primarily a marketing effort aimed at the human comfort need, in this case, "When will I get out?" Although fifty-five minutes

---

2 Arthur W. Hafner, Ph.D., M.B.A, *Pareto's Principle: The 80-20 Rule*, Seton Hall University, http://library.shu.edu

is almost an hour, it doesn't look like an hour. Because the start and end times of the meeting are both within the same one-hour zone, the meeting advertises itself as being short and easy to handle. This is the same principle that retailers use when pricing a $20 item at $19.99 or an $18,000 car at $17,995. A fifty-five-minute event promises to each invitee that before the hour is up, he will be back at his desk or back out on the road where he really wants to be—we are showing him the light at the end of the tunnel.

Ending a meeting before the top of the next hour also allows people to schedule the rest of their day more comfortably. Your guarantee that they'll be back at their desk before the clock strikes the next hour removes the temptation to "squeeze in" a couple of extra calls or activities before the start of the meeting. They know they'll be set free promptly if they arrive promptly, and this makes them more likely to show up on time.

A fixed amount of meeting time, as we observed with keystone time, also encourages focus. People are more likely to stick to an agenda if they know just how much time has been made available. Much can be achieved quickly when the incentive is prompt departure.

The fifty-five-minute meeting is another example of conditioning and influence in action. To promise a meeting under an hour is one thing, but many of your colleagues won't believe it to be possible. However, at the conclusion of your third fifty-five-minute meeting, your reputation will grow—you will have conditioned your people to know that your meetings are quick, productive, and efficient. This, in turn, encourages greater participation and loyalty from your team.

IS THE MEETING NECESSARY AT ALL?

The next time a meeting is called and your attendance is required, or if you are in charge of planning the next meeting, ask yourself first, "Is the meeting necessary?" Could the same information be delivered and the same objective achieved via a telephone conference, a videoconference, or a simple e-mail?

Even if you're not in control of this kind of thing, even if your boss calls the meeting, you can still have influence. You might have an opportunity to inquire as to the objectives of the meeting. (It's called "best practices.") Remember you are doing so in the name of continual improvement for the department and not as a direct challenge to the authority of the person who calls the meeting. It's not what you say, but how you say it.

If conference calls, informal huddles, or well-crafted memos could achieve the same objective as at least some of the meetings, there could be a bottom-line advantage as well. Let's look at the math:

- Take the number of minutes (or hours) taken up by a meeting.
- Multiply by the number of people in attendance.
- Multiply by the estimated average hourly cost of the time of the attendees.
- Double it to account for work they could have been doing instead.

Even using a rough guess, if you estimate the average wage between the most senior and most junior person in attendance as $50 per hour, and if there are ten people in attendance, and if the meeting is an hour long, then the cost of this meeting, including doubling to account for work that could have been done instead, is (1 hour × 10 × 50) × 2 = $1,000.

If you have five meetings a week of this type, then that's $5,000 per week and $260,000 per year.

If, according to the 80/20 rule, only 20 percent of this meeting time is truly productive, then that's $200,000 a year of time and money that could have been spent elsewhere. It may be difficult to question the need for a meeting just on principle, but if you could demonstrate a technique that would save enough money for a new Rolls Royce (or a dozen new company cars), then you might get some attention.

THE AGENDA

If you are the chairperson, then it is to your advantage to prepare an agenda in advance and realistically plan the time allotted for each item. If you are not the chairperson, then ask for a copy of the agenda in advance as a subtle way to teach them how it's done. An agenda is crucial to the successful and profitable running of a meeting. It's a project plan. That sounds pretty straightforward, but many meetings start with only a general idea of what to cover. Others start with an agenda, but fail to set the amount of time allowed for each item.

It is the chairperson's responsibility to think through the meeting before it happens, to identify the topics to be covered, and to list them. It is also the chairperson's responsibility to be realistic as to time—there are only so many things that can be talked about in a given time block.

POP QUIZ–AGENDAS

If you are the chair of the next meeting, and you estimate that each agenda item will be allowed fifteen minutes, how many agenda items could you schedule in fifty-five minutes? The answer is not four, but three. A meeting consists of more than the cut-and-dried agenda items. Opening and closing remarks, questions, housekeeping announcements—these all need time. Keep this quiz in mind, and your meetings will stand a better chance of starting and ending on time.

Here's a sample that allows time for a dynamic, productive, and profitable meeting.

AGENDA
Tuesday the 5th, 10:00A.M.–10:55A.M.
10:00A.M.   Call to order, introduction of meeting officials, housekeeping
10:05A.M.   Item 1 (fifteen minutes)
10:20A.M.   Item 2 (fifteen minutes)
10:35A.M.   Item 3 (fifteen minutes)
10:50A.M.   Summary, action items (five minutes)
10:55A.M.   Closing and adjournment

The *call to order* is an official opening of the meeting. If you have access to a gavel, then it's a great idea to use it. Judges and auctioneers do so for a reason. The sound is audible, unmistakable, and carries great authority. Authority, by the way, is not an endorsement of a power trip. It's to guide people's energy and attention, and reassure them that their time is being respected.

The *meeting officials* should be identified in print in the agenda and aloud during the call to order. Their roles and descriptions as described below should be made clear to everyone around the table.

This agenda should be circulated twenty-four hours in advance, if possible. Doing this has three benefits:

- It allows people to come to the meeting already prepared to discuss the items rather than face them for the first time once the meeting gets underway.
- It is a contract, or a set of ground rules, as to what the meeting will cover and, perhaps more importantly, what it will *not* cover. The agenda need not be circulated for approval or modification, but serves merely as advance notice of the topics to be discussed, and fair warning for all attendees to arrive prepared.
- It's a demonstration of leadership. Prompt distribution of an organized planned agenda sets the tone for the organized, time-efficient meeting to come.
- It's also a demonstration of the respect you have for the participants' time, encouraging greater buy-in and participation.

MEETING OFFICIALS

There are three officials whose presence at a meeting will contribute greatly to its success: the chair, the timekeeper, and the minute-taker.

As *chairperson*, part of your role is to decide not only what will be talked about during the meeting, but how this information will be presented. Will you entertain questions as events unfold, or save them all until the end? Will you allow debate? Is the goal of the meeting to share ideas across the table or to deliver a prepackaged collection of facts? These are the things to decide. They should be mentioned in the agenda and mentioned again during the opening of the meeting.

The *timekeeper* keeps a close eye on the time allotted for each agenda item, uses hand signals to count down the minutes allotted to each agenda item and to each speaker, and ensures that time limits are respected by alerting the group with a gavel. The timekeeper has the authority to keep time and to act as a neutral official of the meeting. This goes a long way in saving face when a participant gets carried away and needs to be reminded when his time is up.

The *minute-taker* takes the notes. These need not be a verbatim transcript, but they should cover:

- the key points raised
- who raised them
- and what is to be done next and by whom (follow-up action items)

The minutes must cover these three points for each agenda item, and if the minute-taker is not clear on any one of them, he has the right to ask and clarify before the meeting adjourns. If the minute-taker is comfortable using a laptop computer or a PDA during the meeting, then minutes can be prepared as the meeting unfolds, ready for distribution immediately upon closure. Minutes should also include the name, phone number/extension, and e-mail address of both the chairperson and the minute-taker in case the need for clarification arises.

RUNNING THE MEETING

Start on time. Starting on time shows respect for people's schedules, and once again exemplifies leadership on the part of the chairperson. Make a point of mentioning what time it is as you begin to demonstrate your willingness to get under way punctually as promised. An on-time start sets a positive note, and adds weight to the promise that the meeting will also end on time. If some of the attendees are guests, the on-time start also reflects extremely well on the company as a whole. Being polite and waiting for someone who is late doesn't carry as much currency as an efficient, on-the-dot kick-off.

If it is the president (or another senior executive) who is late, that's always going to be a judgment call. That person probably has a good excuse for being late, but it is still no excuse for delaying the meeting. If the not-yet-arrived executive is scheduled to deliver the opening speech, then maybe the time could be used for other agenda items. After all, a group of people physically together in one room can either provide a tremendous opportunity to communicate, or can provide a hole in the floor for dollars to drain into. If the executive is merely to be in attendance, and her participation is not necessary to get the meeting under way, then it's probably best to just get started. Consider once again the dollar value of all those people sitting around a boardroom table, biding their time, waiting for the meeting to start. She can always be brought back up to speed at a suitable time after the meeting.

So, right on time, the chairperson calls the meeting to order and then:

- introduces the timekeeper and the minute-taker
- announces when the break times will be
- announces when refreshments will be arriving
- asks all present to silence their cellphones

TOASTMASTERS

If you're interested in learning about and practicing the art of speaking at—and running—meetings, consider visiting your local Toastmasters chapter. Founded in 1924, Toastmasters provides a supportive environment to practice and develop speaking and leadership skills. To find a chapter near you, visit www.toastmasters.org.

Deal only with agenda items. As the meeting progresses, the chairperson sticks to the agenda and to the times allotted for each item. The exception to this rule would be if you are on such a roll with a particular topic that wrapping up would be counterproductive; then obviously you should continue discussing that item until the fiftieth minute. (Remember the Pareto principle—there can always be exceptions.) But even then, mention the time and your desire to modify the agenda before continuing. Keep to the time limits, and use diplomatic but firm instructions if speakers are running overtime or drifting off topic. Once again, a meeting that keeps to an agenda and within time limits is a demonstration of the respect you have for the time and the priorities of the attendees.

Deal with issues separately. In addition to addressing the points of the agenda and having the key thoughts and action items committed to the minutes, meetings will often bring forth other points and ideas not relevant to the agenda, but important all the same. One of the ways to give these points the recognition they deserve without losing control of the meeting is to "park" them on a side-sheet. Some meeting managers plan an extra few minutes at the end of a meeting to discuss the extra items that might come up (sounds a lot like opportunity time, doesn't it?). Others defer these new items to the next meeting's agenda. Don't let off-topic discussions take over if you wish to achieve your current meeting's stated goals.

As each agenda item is concluded, the follow-up activities and/ or next steps should be clearly stated so that all present understand them. A classic source of miscommunication and delay occurs when attendees are reluctant to admit they're not clear on a next step. Merely assuming that everyone knows the next step is never enough. It is the chairperson's responsibility to ensure that each participant leaves the room with a clear understanding of what is to follow. The minute-taker also must understand the next steps, since they will have to be put into the minutes. Having him read back the next-step items from the minutes before the meeting adjourns is a good way to ensure that everyone stays on the level.

End on time. It's great if a meeting can end a few minutes early, but it's awful for everyone if it ends late. Concluding a meeting on schedule is a fulfillment of the contract you distributed in the form of a precirculated agenda. It allows people to plan their days accurately around your meetings, knowing that a promised 10:55A.M. end will indeed occur at 10:55A.M. It is also a welcome relief for those who have attended more than their share of drawn-out gatherings. When wrapping up:

- thank all members for their participation
- remind them to turn their phones back on
- end the meeting on an upbeat note
- make a point of officially drawing the meeting to a close, rather than allowing people to simply shuffle out

Minutes should be prepared and circulated no more than twenty-four hours after the meeting, which means that the minute-taker must allow sufficient time in his own schedule to do this. This is part of the closure phase of project management. (See Chapter 3.)

Invite and dismiss as needed. It makes sense to invite the right people to your meeting, but more often than not, the wrong people get invited, too. Maybe it's tradition to invite the whole group, or maybe it's the fear of putting someone's nose out of joint by not inviting her. Being selective about whom you invite to a meeting need not be an exercise in secrecy and power. Rather, you would be doing everyone a favor by making sure that only those who need to be there are invited. You would be demonstrating respect for the busy schedules of both the invitees and the non-invitees.

Similarly, why should participants have to stay when they are no longer needed? If people have better things to do with their time, perhaps they should be let go after agenda items most relevant to them have been discussed. Meetings should be about productivity, not face-time. The remaining attendees will immediately and unconsciously refocus the energy of the room, allowing greater concentration on the next agenda item. Ensure, however, that all attendees, including those who leave early, are on the list to receive the full minutes of the meeting.

Allow time to vent. Sometimes one of the most productive things to come out of a meeting is a release of pressure. Such a gripe session may not seem at first glance to be the kind of thing needed or wanted at a productive meeting. But remember, when working with humans, there are times when emotional unloading is the only way to get past issues that would otherwise hold up the entire meeting or project. If you suspect there is a need to vent, it's best to schedule it in rather than suppress it further.

HANDLING BACK-TO-BACK MEETINGS

If you have any say in this at all, avoid planning meetings back-to-back. Allow just a little breathing space between them; time to collect your thoughts, follow through on the activities of the previous meeting, and refresh yourself before the next meeting.

Between-meeting breathing space should be used to actually breathe, not to take on additional tasks such as returning phone calls or running back to the office (which simply introduces new preoccupations at a time when you should be focusing on the meeting ahead).

The main principles behind Cool Time is that the mind, body, and soul should be as refreshed, enthused, and energetic as possible. The way to attain this state is to allow time to move from one activity to another without losing mental energy and excellence to the stresses of the day. Even though you might not think you have a great deal of choice in the timing of meetings currently, remember that it takes weeks to modify the habits of an individual or a group. Steadily, over the weeks and months to come, you will be able to influence the timing, structure, and pace of most of the meetings you attend.

However, if you find yourself scheduled into back-to-back meetings, check with both chairpeople as to whether agendas can be accommodated to either allow you to leave the first meeting early, or to join the second meeting intentionally late, in time for agenda item No. 2. Strength comes from flexibility, and opportunity comes from communication.

THE HEALTHY MEETING ENVIRONMENT

Your meeting room is an equal contributor to any successful meeting, and it can do a great deal for the collective health, sanity, and productivity of the participants. Some people hold meetings in rooms where office furniture has come to die, while others use facilities with huge, comfortable chairs and remote-control gadgets that would impress James Bond. What do *you* have available? What *could* you make available? Since we respond so well to creature comforts, anything you can do to enhance the comfort of the human beings around the table will pay off in the form of shorter, more focused, more productive meetings. Wherever and whenever possible, meetings should be scheduled as much around the availability of the optimum room as around the availability of the participants.

First, the most important things—breaks: We're here to meet, to talk, and to come up with good ideas. The first and most important thing on the agenda should therefore be breaks! If you can't keep within the fifty-five-minute limit described earlier—if your meeting is scheduled to last ninety minutes or more—then be absolutely sure to schedule a break on the hour. Humans need breaks.

Breaks do not make meetings longer. They make them shorter overall and more productive by counteracting the sluggishness and distraction that comes from reduced circulation. Breaks allow people to recharge, refresh, stay connected, and come to conclusions more quickly.

And not only does the brain need fresh oxygen, it also works best, as mentioned before, when a finish line is visible. By informing people at the outset of a meeting when the breaks are scheduled, you allow them to budget their patience and energy appropriately. You stand a greater chance of coming to conclusions and agreements by promising them some relief at scheduled times, basically once every hour.

Lighting: If you have the option, choose a room that is lit with natural light. The second choice would be incandescent light (such as recessed pot lights)—anything but fluorescent light. If your room has both, then turn off the fluorescent ones. Incandescent lighting is easier on the eyes, allowing attendees to remain alert without inducing either sleepiness because a room is too dark, or eye fatigue and headaches because the fluorescent lighting flickers. Also, if one end of the room will be used for delivering a presentation, ensure that you have separate lighting controls that allow the presenter and the material to be adequately lit without either drowning out a projected display or leaving the presenter in darkness. Lighting controls should be clearly marked so that they can be controlled smoothly and correctly, not only by you but also by whomever you might ask to dim/turn on the lights for you. Any time you can book a boardroom with a window, do it. The human metabolism craves natural light, and even when the blinds are drawn for a presentation, the presence of natural light so close by provides energy and stamina for the attendees. Whenever possible, keep the blinds open to allow the natural light to flood the room.

Air circulation: Good air helps keep people charged and invigorated. Meetings that last longer than twenty minutes risk losing the attention of the attendees if good air is not available. This means choosing a meeting room that has either windows that open (a rare find, perhaps) or a manually controlled air conditioning/fan system. Locate the manual temperature control, and set the temperature of the room to about 68°F (20°C), which is cool without being cold. Since people react to heat and cold differently, it is essential to ask how they are feeling during the meeting. On the whole, it's better to have a room a little on the cool side than overly warm. If meetings go on for hours, or if the room is booked for back-to-back meetings throughout the day, you might want to consider using a humidifier or ionizer to help maintain air quality.

CHURCHES AND TEMPLES

For centuries, churches and temples have stood as outstanding examples of the power of effective meeting spaces. Their architecture is intended to inspire the appropriate feelings from their congregations. The air is scented and the lights are warm and colorful, all to provide an enhanced sensory experience. And, perhaps most importantly, the entrances are always at the end farthest from the altar to accommodate latecomers without distraction.

Noise: Noise distracts. A meeting is supposed to be an exercise in communication and education, and too much noise will distract attendees from your message. The hiss that comes from heating/air systems, projection systems, overhead projectors, and computers is called white noise, which imposes itself upon the hearing and attention of your invitees. When you assess a meeting room, stand perfectly still and listen for white noise. Check the sound level when the air circulation fan is on. Check the "distraction factor" when the air circulation system shuts off and then turns on again. Will this noise be too much of a disturbance, or can you work around it? Will there be noise from other meeting rooms? If two meeting rooms are separated by a removable wall and the person speaking in the adjoining meeting has a powerful voice, or there is laughter, applause, or the sound of movement, these distractions will be counterproductive to your meeting, especially if the meeting next door seems to be more fun. Check with the person who books meeting rooms and look for one that is as isolated as possible. Will there be noise from traffic outside, or construction/renovation within the building? Is there a fire drill scheduled for that day? Again, find out about these possibilities from the appropriate sources before booking your room.

Phones: At the opening of the meeting, ask that all cellphones be set on "silent," so that calls can still get through, and people can excuse themselves to take the call if they must without disturbing the other attendees too much. It is advisable to have the same message printed on the agenda.

Seating: Since most people spend much of their meeting time sitting down, comfortable chairs are a must. Why is this important to time management? Because people who are uncomfortable or in pain will not be at their best, which results in delay, reduced participation, or even absenteeism. If you have the choice and opportunity, choose a meeting room with comfortable chairs that support correct posture and alignment. Remove those that squeak, even if you have to do so while the meeting is in progress.

Refreshments: They're more than just welcome at meetings, they're essential. Coffee and tea are standards, but to ensure that your participants remain refreshed and hydrated, keep plenty of water on hand. Ask for cold water, of course, but if you can, leave out the ice cubes as they are too distracting when poured into a glass. Food is also useful. Remember, however, that the "fun" foods, such as doughnuts and pastries, are full of empty calories that do nothing to provide stamina for the rest of the meeting, and in fact will result in sluggishness as soon as the sugar has burned off. Consider low-fat muffins and fresh fruit, high-water content vegetables such as carrots and celery, and small sandwiches if a real lunch needs to be served. Avoid foods high in fat, such as pizza, and those that are high in carbohydrates or starch, such as pasta salad and potatoes, if you plan to work on challenging topics after lunch.

ALTERNATE MEETING STRATEGIES

Formalized meetings in boardrooms are not always the only approach.

Stealth and pouncing: When it comes to small, two-person meetings, such as between you and a colleague or manager, if there is a way to avoid having to hold the meeting at all yet still get the information across correctly, then consider pouncing. Many great meetings and results have come from informal encounters in kitchenettes, hallways, and elevators, in which the pouncer comes prepared with suitable questions or points prepared during the morning I-Beam Review, which can be delivered quickly and casually.

Coffee shops: People have been meeting to talk business in coffee shops for 500 years. Why stop now? Unless your topic is of a highly sensitive or confidential nature, a two-, four-, or eight-person meeting in the local coffee establishment can be a vibrant, productive trip, and a refreshing change.

Successful meetings, then, are an example of influence in action. The discussions and ideas that come from the meeting are its primary goal perhaps, but the work of getting people to the table and keeping them alert is based in your knowledge of the inner motivations of the human being.

But what happens when they drop in to meet you at your desk?

CHAPTER 9
INTERRUPTIONS AND INTERACTIONS: DEALING WITH THE PEOPLE IN YOUR WORLD

Certainly one of the most challenging areas of time management is dealing with the people with whom you share your work space. In Chapter 5 we saw how regular huddles with the boss might keep lines of communication and expectation clear. But what about when someone calls or drops in, either with relevant information or just to shoot the breeze? In this chapter, we'll combine what we have seen in the previous chapters on influence and keystone time/payback time with some new techniques to keep these conversations under control.

In Chapter 3 we discussed how the secret behind memorizing people's names was to *remember* to use word association, thus turning an uncontrolled activity into a controlled, proactive one. People trapped in conversations are often caught in that uncontrolled moment, wishing the conversation would end (or that it had not happened at all) but finding themselves immobilized by the rules of politeness. It takes great courage of conviction to tell someone to go away, and it's certainly not advisable to do so to customers, even the long-winded ones.

BOXING THE CONVERSATION: ENTRANCE AND EXIT LINES

Phone calls are a great example of uncontrolled, time-eating moments, since live conversations generally progress freely and organically, usually well beyond their usefulness.

However, it need not be so if you establish boundaries at the outset as to how long the conversation should take. Consider starting a conversation with an entrance line such as, "Bill, it's great to hear from you. I have just four minutes until my teleconference. What can I do for you?" *When said correctly*, this establishes a parameter for the call, and places the focus and good feeling back upon the caller. Notice the two key phrases:

- *I have just four minutes* guides the caller and informs him how much time is available to talk. This is a mini-meeting agenda that says "This meeting should last for four minutes; let's begin."
- *What can I do for you?* keeps the tone positive, implying your willingness to help under the time condition just set.

Then, as the call progresses, you can deploy similar, correctly phrased exit lines, such as "I must go—my teleconference is starting now" to wrap up the call without causing offense (even if you don't have a teleconference to go to).

Some people have trouble with the idea of making up half-truths to end conversations, while others do not. Therefore, the phrases that you choose to use must be the type that you can live with and say with conviction. Suggestions might include:

- I've got a meeting in four minutes.
- My boss is waiting for me.
- My other line is ringing.
- I'm covering for someone else right now.
- My cellphone battery is almost gone.
- A customer just walked in.
- Let's pick this up again in a couple of days—how's Friday for you?

The point is that with so many calls being made and received each day, a great amount of time is lost to the impromptu nature of free-flowing conversation. By establishing ground rules for the call, both at the beginning and at its conclusion, using socially acceptable excuses and a positive emotion throughout, you will be able to keep most calls to a reasonable, manageable, and predictable length. The benefits of this technique include:

- getting to the point of the conversation more quickly
- spending less time on the phone
- balancing good relationships with efficient timing
- attaining heightened accuracy when it comes to calculating the predicted durations of phone calls as part of your I-Beam Review

And, yes, there are certain calls to which this technique does not apply—with a key client, for example, or with your boss. That's why we discussed the 80/20 rule in Chapter 7. The idea is not to apply these principles to every single one of your calls and interactions, but if you can apply them to *most*, you'll be much further ahead than if you did nothing at all.

DEALING WITH THE DROP-IN VISITOR

Many people work in exposed, open-concept areas in which workplaces are defined by cubicles. Some share desks. For the majority of these workers, their object of daytime lust is an office with a door. "At least then," they say, "I can get some work done." Yet if they were to talk with the people who actually *had* doors, they'd find in most cases that the door is ineffective for one or more of the following reasons:

- People walk in anyway.
- People slip memos under the door.
- People slip memos under the door and then send an e-mail about the memo they've just sent.
- You're rendered defenseless by the company's open-door policy.

When people are the source of your distraction, the dilemma is how to maintain an appearance of approachability while not becoming a habitual victim of time theft. This balancing act is difficult. Our desire to appear available, effective, enthusiastic, and approachable forces us to inversely prioritize—to place the needs of our colleagues before our own. We often do this without thinking. We do it to be polite, or simply to blend in with the existing corporate culture. We let it happen to us because there seems to be no other way. That's when it's time to use the "intelligent push-back" to retaliate and place your priorities first.

When a colleague sticks his head in the door and says, "Have you got a minute?" what do you say? If you respond to this question by saying, "Sure, come on in. What can I do for you?" you may think you're saying, "I'm approachable and capable. I'm a good professional," but what you're actually saying is, "Sure, your time is more valuable than mine—go ahead and use up as much as you want." You are allowing a visitor's time and priorities to take precedence over your own. As soon as you allow someone to chisel into your block of time, you are giving up things that cannot be won back. In truth, you don't want to actually engage this person in a conversation since you're already too busy, but you also do not want to cause anger or hurt feelings by rejecting him outright. Nor do you want to appear unapproachable or unfriendly to the office community. And, of course, a "minute" never actually takes a minute. So, what can you do? Well, here are a few ideas:

Remind him of your payback time. This is the time reserved after keystone time to deal specifically with his requests with your undivided attention. (See Chapter 6.)

Use the sixty-second qualifier. As discussed in Chapter 6, if his question is such that it can be answered in under 60 seconds, then of course you'll hear it, but if it will take longer, perhaps he should come back during payback time. (Remember, these are the kinds of things that should be introduced first at a "best practices" meeting, so that your colleagues can get used to the concepts before being confronted by them.)

Have entrance and exit lines ready. This will guide the length of the interaction and provide you with an acceptable way out. Exit lines do not need to be just about upcoming meetings or phone calls. For drop-in visitors who are particularly difficult to dislodge:

- give them some filing to do during the conversation
- start packing up some documents and clearing your desk to go somewhere—to the copier or, as a last resort, the rest room

Deflect and save face. Even if you're not in keystone time, when a colleague wants a moment of your time right away, provide him with an alternate time for the discussion. An answer to the original question, "Have you got a minute?", could instead sound like this: "Well, at the moment I'm in the middle of this work, but I will come to see you at 11:15." In this way you are guaranteeing the interrupter your undivided attention at a later time, not too far away. You are demonstrating respect for your colleague's comfort concerns and, most importantly, you are helping that person save face by deflecting him from your current activities without being insulting.

It is crucial, however, that you follow up on your promise in this scenario. If you say 11:15, then you *must* visit your colleague at that time.

Incidentally, whenever you use this technique, make a habit of becoming the visitor rather than inviting your colleague to return to your work space at 11:15. Why? Whenever you make the visitation, you are at liberty to end it whenever you want—you remain in control. When the visitor comes to you, getting him to leave your work space in a timely manner may become an additional challenge.

If you think the deflect-and-save-face technique is truly unworkable, think of other professional people from whom this behavior is already expected: company presidents and senior officials, dentists, doctors, and lawyers. These types of people seldom have time for you the moment you call—they work by appointment. Wouldn't you be more than a little surprised, perhaps even a little concerned, if your own doctor answered the phone when you called? Seeing the people who need to see you by appointment is a profitable and efficient use of your time. If it sounds snooty and stuck-up to you at this moment, remember that when properly applied, it demonstrates a professional talent for prioritization while maintaining approachability and accessibility with colleagues. It's all in how you tell people. It's not necessary to be mean or objectionable when declining a person's drop-in visit. "No" is a lot easier to pronounce when it is followed up with an alternative time for discussion:

Interrupter:	Hi. Got a minute?
You:	Well, at this moment, Bob, I'm just in the middle of this report. I have half an hour left. How's 11:15 for you?

- *Don't feel you have to explain too much.* If you answer no to the "Got a minute?" question, and then follow that up with too many specifics, such as "I'm working on the Johnson report right now," you are opening up a bargaining position in which the interrupter may assess the importance of the Johnson report against that of his own request, and then gain the upper hand by deciding that his own request is of higher priority for both of you, leaving you with little room to put forth a second objection. Do not volunteer any information that may weaken your position. Talk only about that which will help to communicate the win–win scenario.

- *Keep your I-Beam Agenda nearby and reachable.* In those situations where you have no choice but to elaborate on why you don't have the time to entertain a visitor, your complete, up-to-date I-Beam Agenda demonstrates your schedule for the day in black and white, proving that you really are quite busy. It is far more credible than trying to recite a general description of your scheduled events from memory.

- *Always handle your deflect-and-save-face response with care and discretion.* Certain people, especially senior managers, may hold priorities that truly are higher than the work you are doing, and they therefore should be seen right away. Like all the suggestions in this book, use sensitivity and judgment in determining your priorities and framing your answers.

If the visitor insists on speaking right then and there, use your entrance and exit strategies to keep the discussion inside a fixed box of time.

Come back in sixty ... An alternative to establishing a time for visitors to return, as in the deflect-and-save-face technique above, is to simply suggest that they come back in sixty minutes. In many cases, the issue or question that the visitors have won't last that long. They will either:

- find another person to ask
- solve the problem themselves
- forget about the problem altogether

Not every issue and crisis in this world needs to be dealt with right away, and sometimes getting stuck on an insignificant issue will leave you unavailable for your own work.

Whether you choose to politely accommodate all requests or instead deploy some of the techniques above, either way, you will be conditioning people. They will learn how they can behave with you based on how you treat them. It is too easy to build a reputation as someone who can be visited at the convenience of the visitor. If people learn they can drop in on you at any time and spend as much time as they want, it will keep happening and you will not get any work done. Remember the 80/20 rule. Instead of trying to eliminate 100 percent of the interrupters from your life, seek instead to deflect 80 percent of them.

Finally, don't allow interruptions to be a proxy for procrastination. Almost any diversion is welcome when you're faced with an undesirable task. Unfortunately, the task will still be there after your visitor has left, and all you'll have achieved is the loss of several minutes of your workday.

BODY LANGUAGE

A great deal of the messages sent from one human to another are done through body language. The eyes, the posture, the subconscious way we position our bodies speaks to people in ways they're not always aware of. Body language can be used to encourage or discourage drop-in visitors. Conscious awareness of the messages you broadcast to your colleagues will change your position from that of a candid participant in such a discussion to an active controller of the relationship.

Keep your body facing your work. Whatever type of task you are working on, keep the central plane of your body directly focused on the work. Shoulders, eyes, and hands should all face the work itself, offering no overture. As an example of this, try an experiment: Sit in a chair that has arms or supports on either side on which you can rest your elbows. Imagine that the work you have to do is in front of you on a computer screen or within easy reach on a desk directly in front of you. With your elbows resting on the arms of the chair, steeple your fingers (bring both hands together as in prayer) and extend your neck forwards a little so that your lips touch the index fingers of your steepled hands. Stare at the work in front of you. Feel the forward momentum of your posture. Your whole body is in central alignment with the task in front of you, and a passer-by would pick up on this. Now try the opposite. Lean back in the chair, tilt your head upwards a little, and rub your jawline with one hand, while extending the other arm out across the desk. Feel how open your upper body becomes. The extension of one arm and the tilted head offers an open space for a drop-in visitor to read as available, a nonthreatening place to enjoy some socialization.

Avoid eye contact. Concentrated focus on a task also eliminates chance eye contact. Remember from Chapter 2 that we are hardwired to observe movements and changes within our field of view. It is extremely difficult to avoid wanting to look at someone as he passes by—curiosity demands it. But eye contact is the ultimate invitation, and not only does it pull people in, it sets a precedent, it conditions your visitor to see your work zone as a social area, one he will return to again and again.

Use props. Headphones send a powerful message. Many people have described to me how they use a telephone headset to achieve privacy. They're not actually talking to anyone on the phone, just wearing it. Visitors are likely to pull up short and go elsewhere if they perceive that you're on the phone. Regular headphones, too, if they're allowed in your workplace (and if they're not, you'd still have a strong case for them, using the "best practices" technique described in Chapter 14), not only deflect people who might otherwise pounce on you, they're also an excellent way to increase your productivity during focused keystone time by creating a cone of concentration. (See Chapter 6.)

Similarly, if the dual concept of keystone time and payback time has been properly introduced into your community via a best practices meeting (a.k.a. collective conditioning), then any symbol, such as a squeeze ball or a Mickey Mouse pencil sharpener, could serve as a deflector, symbolizing that you're in keystone time. So long as the visitor is aware of when keystone time ends, the body language of Mickey himself can be enough to keep your peace intact.

Minimize your moves. If it's too late, and the drop-in visitor has already made himself comfortable in your work zone, then minimize the movements you use to greet him. Rather than sitting back fully in your chair to engage in an open chat, just raise your eyes and eyebrows, or look over the tops of your glasses. Keep your body "closed in" over your work.

Keep your hands poised over your keyboard or writing. Let him know, without having to say so verbally, that you do not intend to stop what you are doing. Don't let go of the pen, the mouse, or the focused posture.

ON THE RUN

As soon as you leave your work space, you become fair game for getting pounced on by others, either for ad hoc meetings or for small talk. The formula to getting from A to B without interruption is: Walk fast, carry papers, look worried.

SOCIAL SITES

The idea behind defensive body language is not to turn anyone into a hermit. There are times for socializing and there are times for focus. Both are beneficial. However, conditioning, as we have seen, is conditioning no matter what you do. When the time comes that you need a break and you consider your drop-in visitor to be a welcome and timely diversion, it is wise to walk with this person to another place—the kitchenette, the copy machine, a location other than your work zone—so that he can associate the social interaction with that location rather than your work space. This also gives the added benefit of having control over the closure of the conversation rather than waiting for him to leave your cubicle.

HOW TO SAY NO

When a colleague or superior asks you or tells you to take on an additional task, many people feel it would be very difficult, embarrassing, or dangerous to say no. However, saying yes can be just as dangerous to you and just as disappointing eventually to the requestor. It means you may end up working too hard on too many projects, and the quality of all of them will suffer.

The ability to say no to additional tasks starts by redefining the term "no" so that it is no longer a term of rejection but one of guidance in which the requestor sees the merit in seeking out someone else.

- *If you feel obliged to say yes because he is standing in front of you*: Make sure your I-Beam Agenda is up-to-date and visible. This gives you a tangible tool of negotiation. When your requestor can actually see the work you already have to do, it helps to put his request in perspective.

- *If you know you are too busy*: Communicate clearly that in saying no now, you are giving him the opportunity to save time by looking for another resource rather than finding out later that the task cannot be finished on time. Even people with the best intentions find out too late that it can't all get done. This is an application of the "pay me now or pay me later" rule, which says that it's better to get the "bad" news up front than to come back later and get it when time has run out.

- *If you feel obliged to say yes because you are a nurturing person willing to help others*: Remember that there has to be a line in the sand somewhere. Whatever you do or say, you will be conditioning this person, and his expectations will be based on how you respond. Once you say yes, the precedent will have been set, and he will expect a yes on each subsequent request. His behavior will also modify itself. He will no longer feel the need to find other resources or to time his activities to anything but the last minute, knowing you will always be there at the rescue. It's a situation that will only worsen with time.

- *If you feel obliged to say yes because it's something you can do, even though it's not part of your regular job*: Be very careful. The road to Hell, as they say, is paved with good intentions. Once other tasks get prioritized before your regular tasks, either your manager will find out and ask why this is or, worse, you will have just "yessed" yourself into an additional set of responsibilities without getting paid for them. Your abilities in this second area, once known, will relieve the department of having to hire a replacement, and the tasks will remain yours.

- *If you feel obliged to say yes because a friend is in a bind*: There is certainly nothing wrong with helping someone in trouble, but there must be closure. After accommodating his request once, be sure to huddle with this person and explain how he might modify his plans next time so that this need not happen again.

- *If you feel obliged to say yes because it's your boss who's making the request*: It's probably best to accommodate the request, but make sure to bring it up at the next huddle so the two of you can identify a suitable alternative.

- *If you feel obliged to say yes because you feel uncomfortable in confrontational situations*: This becomes a conflict management issue. One of the basic rules of conflict management is that you take the "you" out of the conflict—remove the emotion and focus on the facts. Eliminate the idea that you are rejecting another person, and focus simply on the facts of what can and cannot be done. "Here's my schedule, here's what I am expected to do right now, here's where I have some time, and here's where I do not." Even though you use the word "I," the focus of the conversation is the agenda, the workload, and the requestor's relationship to it.

- *If you feel obliged to say yes because the requestor is being overly imposing:* Put it this way: "If you want me to drop everything in order to accommodate your request, I will, but keep in mind that I will have to do the same thing for the next person who comes along and asks the same question."

- *If you feel obliged to say yes because it's part of your job, but you're too busy at the moment*: Use the "Come back in sixty" technique above (see page 114). This is not actually saying yes or no, but simply deflecting the request for an hour, during which time it might resolve itself. Or offer an alternate time. Though this is not actually saying no, it is saying, "Not right now," which gives you both the chance to book an acceptable alternative time to do the work.

Then, of course, once you've gotten rid of your drop-in visitors and their requests, you can finally get back to work. Oh, but wait a minute—that red light on your phone is flashing again.

CHAPTER 10
COMMUNICATING: GETTING
THE MESSAGE

THE PHONE

The phone as a business communications tool has evolved quite significantly from a black rotary dial desk set to today's ultra-portable wireless units, but in many cases the approach to using one has not. It is still viewed by many as the tool of the immediate: *Someone wants to talk to me, so I'd better answer.* It also happens in reverse: *I want to talk, but I'm just getting voicemail, so I'm feeling frustrated.*

The fact is that the odds of actually connecting with people "live" are getting fewer and fewer with each passing day. As a caller we must approach each call with two prepared mindsets: What to say if we get a live person who answers, and what to say if we get voicemail. Most people, however, don't approach the call with two mindsets, just the one: *What I'm going to say when the person I'm calling picks up.* It's the urgency of the moment. When we find they're not there, we are forced to leave a voicemail, which seems like a poor alternate.

VOICEMAIL: THE ULTIMATE CUSTOMER-RELATIONS TOOL

The greatest thing to ever happen to voice communication is voicemail, which, when correctly used, carries messages and delivers guidance patiently and reliably.

However, many people don't see it that way. They see voicemail as an apologist, one that says to the caller, "I'm really sorry, but I'm not here right now. Will you accept this poor substitute instead?" They communicate such a sentiment by way of a tired unchanging message that goes something like this: "Hi, you've reached Steve. I'm either away from my desk or on the other line right now. So please leave a message at the tone."

Such a greeting does little to soothe the caller's fears of the un-known. It leaves the caller high and dry. *Is Steve actually in today? Will he return my call soon? How will I know? How much further has this got me in my efforts to complete my tasks?* The high-and-dry greeting becomes a self-fulfilling prophecy, inspiring the caller to leave an equally bland message such as: "Hi, Steve, it's Pat. Can you call me when you get in? Thanks." Or, worse, they press 0 to get someone to hunt you down.

Guide your callers and manage their expectations. A far better alter-native is to satisfy your callers' need to communicate with you, and to transfer positive sentiment and guidance by ensuring that your out-bound greeting contains the following:

- *Today's date:* This reassures them that as of today you are still alive and working for the company. Whether you are at your desk or just checking in from elsewhere, you are available and accessible. This means changing your greeting daily.
- *That they have permission to leave a detailed message:* Some people are hesitant to leave long messages for fear of inconveniencing you, or running out of message time and getting beeped. Let them know that you appreciate detailed messages and are happy to receive them.
- *That you will be returning calls at or by a certain time today:* Obviously, this deals with their fear of the unknown, but, more importantly, removes the need for them to keep calling back while you're busy with other things.
- *That you will be available to give them your undivided attention at that time:* This is an example of the positive payback.
- *That you are upbeat, energetic, and happy to hear from them:* Though

this may sound overly sentimental, remember that people are conditioned not only through actions but also through perceptions. We are always more eager to cooperate with someone who sounds positive and conciliatory than we are with someone who sounds drab and depressed.

This allows for a message like this, for example:

You've reached Steve Prentice of ABC Company at extension 123 for Tuesday the 16th. I will be in a meeting this morning and will be returning calls after 11:00. Please feel free to leave a detailed voice message of up to two minutes, and I will get back to you as promised. If this message is urgent, please press 0 to reach my assistant. Thank you.

- Stating your name clearly identifies yourself to any callers who may have been bounced to your inbox by an operator.
- Stating your extension (if you have one) serves a similar purpose. If a caller has asked the switchboard operator for you by name, he is often patched through without being informed of the extension. By identifying your extension in your message, you enable the caller to update his records and make it unnecessary for him to spell out your first or last name on the keypad.
- By offering an additional opportunity by way of dialing 0 for the switchboard or assistant, you offer another alternative. This helps reduce the sense of urgency many callers have that their message must be attended to immediately. When they themselves have to decide whether the call should go through to an assistant, most of them (80 percent) will recognize that the message is not a life-or-death matter, and will be even more accepting of your voicemail options.

The main objective of such a substantive voicemail greeting is to ensure that communication continues in your absence, and that the callers' expectations are managed by way of a reasonable alternative to the immediate; that is, a return call from you just after 11:00. This frees you up to attend meetings, deal with clients, and use keystone time to your full advantage, returning calls when it is both appropriate and convenient.

Of course, the success of this technique, just as with keystone time and payback time, is to ensure you follow up on the promise and pay your caller back. Your greeting sets up a contract, which, when fulfilled by your return call, will start a positive conditioning process: The caller will learn that he can rely on prompt callback. His stress is replaced by reassurance. He is free to get on with the rest of the day, knowing that the next step in this particular relationship is in place, while you retain greater control over your time. Once you get into the habit of returning calls within a set timeframe, your callers will be amazed and grateful. What seems like a two-hour delay to you is seen by most as a prompt response. You win twice: You get to keep your time for other things, and you still appear as a customer-focused hero.

Here are a couple of final points regarding your outbound greeting:

- *Speak slowly.* Let your message convey the Cool approach to managing time and priorities.
- *Use an upbeat voice.* Notice in the example above that there was no need to end the greeting with "… and have a wonderful day," unless that is your style already. However, recording your greeting using a normal conversational tone *will* result in a dull and monotonous greeting. Do what the radio announcers do and use a voice that is a little bouncier and varied than you might use when talking face to face. This will compensate for the leveling effect of the phone system's electronics and will deliver an upbeat, positive, and credible set of instructions to your caller.

One final point: There are certainly some types of professionals for whom answering the phone immediately is part of the job—receptionists, for example, or traders and brokers. Naturally, putting off calls for an hour or two would be counterproductive, but it might still be possible for you to use this technique for those minutes you'll need to have for short meetings, lunch, and one of the most pressing calls of all, the call of nature.

USING CALL DISPLAY TO MAXIMUM ADVANTAGE

This is pretty straightforward, but still underused. If you don't know who's calling, you have the right not to answer. Call display gives you the opportunity to decide rather than react, to answer only the highest-priority callers—the top 20 percent—those whose importance outweighs the importance of the work in front of you, and to leave the rest for later. If you've ever stayed in a hotel, you know that a peephole in the door allows you the choice of whether to admit a visitor or not. Maybe you have one in the main door to your home. It's a tool for personal security. Call display is your tool for time security.

As with all of the techniques in this book, it's your choice as to how to implement them. If you are in sales, and you fear that passing up an unknown call may jeopardize a sale, then you may opt to take the call, in which case having your entrance and exit lines ready will at least allow you to control the call's duration. But there's always the "in-a-meeting" technique as well. What if you were in a meeting with a client when this new call comes in? Would you interrupt a meeting with a client to take a call from another client or prospect? Usually, that other caller would go to voicemail anyway, and you would get back to them pretty quickly. The strength of your outbound voicemail greeting would let them know you're near, and your prompt return call will impress them all the more. Since they would go to voicemail anyway, the technique of passing over unknown incoming calls to avoid interruption, paired with a prompt callback for high-priority callers, has merit as a Cool way to stay productive and balance priorities.

One common argument is that call display is OK if the display identifies the caller by name, but what if it's just a phone number that appears? If you're waiting for return calls, keep a written list of the phone numbers of those you've called as the "hot-button-pick-up-now" numbers. If you've left a message for John at 212-555-1234 and he's one of your top 20 percent of callers whom you're willing to take immediately, then keep that number near the call-display screen.

LEAVING MESSAGES TO MAXIMUM ADVANTAGE

When you make a call and you get someone else's voicemail, that's not a dead end, either. Quite the opposite. It's an opportunity to continue communicating efficiently, to change from *telephone tag* to *telephone hockey*, in which knowledge is passed back and forth toward a goal.

Remember the "two-mindset" concept above. When you call, be equally prepared to leave a substantive message as you would if you were to talk live. Make a point. Be substantive.

- Prepare a point-form list of discussion items before calling, and use this as the agenda for your call. This works equally well for live conversations. Address each point clearly and concisely before moving onto the next point, especially with regard to what actions your "callee" should take. If your message will be a long one, inform the listener accordingly, such as, "Pat, in this message I have five key points to make and it should take about two minutes." This gives your recipient greater choice as to whether to listen now or at a time when she can take notes and respond appropriately.
- Leave your name and company name at the start of your message, and announce that you'll be leaving the contact number at the end. Avoid giving out your phone info at the start because your callee may still be foraging for a pen and, more importantly, you want him to actually listen to your message. It is unwise to announce your phone number in the middle of the message. If your callee needs to replay your message to hear the number again, it can be frustrating to have to search back through to find it. If it's at the very end he'll need to replay only the very last few seconds. The start of your message might begin like this: "Hi, Pat, this is Steve Prentice from ABC Company. I will leave you my phone number at the end of this message, but what I want to talk to you about is ..." If this all sounds like a lot of kid-gloves treatment, remember that influencing people comes not from force but from awareness of a person's inner motivations. It's unlikely someone will ever say to you, "You have a really proactive voicemail style, and that's why I do business

with you." But they will pick up on the way you make life easier for them in small measures, and living creatures are always attracted to things that make them feel good and safe.

- When announcing your name and company name, pronounce them clearly, especially if this is your first time communicating with this particular callee. That sounds obvious, but many people rush through the essential contact info because they've heard themselves say it so many times.

WHEN NOTHING BUT LIVE WILL DO

For those times when you really need to talk live and voicemail is just not enough, you can still use voicemail to set an appointment. For example, leave a message for your elusive contact that gives three times during which you guarantee that you will be available and waiting. The message could go along these lines:

> Pat, it's Steve. We've been playing telephone tag for a couple of days now, and I really think we should chat. I will be available between 2:00p.m. and 2:30p.m. on Wednesday, 4:00p.m. and 6:00p.m. on Thursday, and 9:00a.m. and 10:00a.m. on Friday. Let's set a date to talk. Leave me a message today by voicemail or e-mail letting me know which one of these times is good for you, and I'll set the appointment. My number is …

Set an appointment time to meet on the phone, just as you would to meet in person. Schedule it accordingly, and respect its sanctity. Make sure you are there to receive the call at the given time, and do not take any other calls. By keeping your appointments in this fashion, your reputation as a reliable, accessible professional will flourish, even while you administer your time on your own terms.

RECORD EVERYTHING

One of the benefits of working in Cool Time is that nothing will get past you. Time, information, or opportunity—they're yours to grab and keep. So take notes after every call or voicemail—primarily to keep a record of activities, ideas, and commitments made during the communication—but also to create a history. All of your calls taken or made for an entire year or more, or all of the calls for a specific project, can be stored in one searchable document and safely backed up.

STEALTH MESSAGING AFTER HOURS

A great way of maximizing your call-returning efforts while minimizing the time involved is to return calls after hours as a series of thirty- to sixty-second voicemails all sent after the close of business.

Though Cool Time generally disfavors working during family or personal time, let's look at the math. If you have twenty calls to return, and it's 4:00 p.m., and if the substance of these calls does not involve the need for a conversation, just one-way information from you, then by returning these calls during business hours, you risk getting trapped in nonessential conversations (small talk). Even if these twenty calls were limited to five minutes each, you would now be on the hook for 100 extra minutes at the office—over an hour and a half. If, however, you took these calls home with you and you made them one after the other, they could take no more than one minute each—fifteen seconds to dial and connect, thirty seconds to record, and fifteen seconds to mark it down as done (follow-through). That's a total of twenty minutes, and you would have arrived home in time for dinner.

And if you feel that leaving messages at 9:00 p.m. would create an impression in your callee's mind that you're working too many late hours, consider using an opening script like this:

> Pat, hi, it's Steve. I'm not working late. I'm just saving your time and mine by returning your call promptly and leaving you a quick message for you to pick up tomorrow morning...

That's the Cool Time approach: Defending your time, while keeping your callers happy, choosing which callers you want to talk to in real time, and knowing how to stay in control all the way along.

E-MAIL

As mentioned in Chapter 2, our reaction to incoming e-mail is a conditioned reflex based on a need to answer the urgency of the "You've got mail" icon, a condition I call Answerholism. This means that we often answer e-mail before it's truly necessary because we feel we have to.

To add to that, a great deal of internal e-mail is sent before it's really ready to be sent. People are under such pressure to move to the next thing on their own packed agenda that they pass work along, or send FYI's to save time in having to summarize key points and expectations. This is a classic update of the Harvard Business School's Monkey principle, which points out that every time someone passes a task off to you, it's another monkey off his back and onto yours.[1] E-mail is the perfect pipeline for these monkeys.

Maureen Malanchuk points out in her book *Inforelief* that we are not in a state of information overload so much as "non-information overload," which has a shorter and dangerously counterproductive shelf life. You may be CC'd on an e-mail today, only to be CC'd on an edited and updated e-mail tomorrow. The time spent checking the first e-mail is wasted. Ambiguity takes the place of concrete communication. Copious amounts of "immature information" demand our attention and waste our limited time.[2]

Then there's internal spam—the general announcements, the thank-you notes, the irrelevant but-oh-so-easy-to-mass-mail corporate noise. As innocuous as the latter may seem, hundreds of studies conducted all around the world have quantified how many thousands of hours and dollars are lost every day as people struggle with this avalanche.

Finally, there's the issue of productivity. Though e-mail serves well as a direct messaging device to confirm meetings and deliver short ideas, it is not so versatile as a medium for creative thought. It creates a type of "silo-mentality" that sabotages creativity. For example, if you were to send me an e-mail asking for my thoughts on an upcoming

---

1 William Oncken, Jr., *Managing Management Time: Who's Got the Monkey?* (Englewood Cliffs, New Jersey: Prentice-Hall, 1984).
2 Maureen Malanchuk, *Inforelief: Stay Afloat in the Infoflood* (San Francisco: Jossey-Bass Publishers, 1996), p. 27.

project, I might pound away for a half-hour or more, creating a long-winded monologue. However, if I were to pick up the phone and talk to you about it, or better yet, set up a time for a really quick meeting, I might observe things in your tone of voice, body language, even in the office around us that would add to my understanding of the situation and influence my thoughts, possibly arriving at a workable solution more quickly. That's where the value of Cool Time comes in: though on the surface e-mail *seems* quicker than a meeting, it may be the meeting that gets more done more effectively through the dynamics of human interaction. Just like Chuko Liang in Chapter 7, it takes a cool head to identify opportunity where others see trouble.

If your workplace does not have an e-mail policy, it's time to get one. Many organizations have rules in place to deal with inappropriate content or personal use of e-mail and the web, but few have an actual, up-to-date user's guide for time-efficient day-to-day use. Here are some suggestions:

Subject line summary: The subject line of an e-mail message should always summarize the entire message and, when necessary, provide additional information. This ensures the entire message gets to the recipient's brain within seconds. Any time you can inform someone instantly, rather than waiting for her to open the e-mail and read the body of the message, you save time—a few seconds, maybe, but more and more as hours, days, and weeks pass.

The same goes when replying to a letter. When people simply hit the "Reply" button and send back a message whose subject line is identical to the original with just an extra *Re:* added, it does nothing to further the communication. However, when you add your own message to the *Re:* line, you create a clear communication that not only talks directly to the recipient immediately, but also becomes a clear part of the "history" when all these e-mails get stored together in a designated project folder. Posterity, as we have seen, has great influence on the future.

Here's a simple example:

My e-mail subject line says: Lunch Thursday?
Yours says: Lunch Thursday?—How's 1:00P.M.?
Mine replies: Lunch Thursday?—How's 1:00P.M.—Great! I'll make reservations

Though subject line space is admittedly limited, the message gets through. The body of the letter may provide additional support details, but the recipient should not have to open the mail to learn what you actually have to say. It also helps your letter stand out from the rest of the pack in your recipient's in-box, thus increasing the chances of it being dealt with promptly.

Update your CC distribution policy: Ensure that only the right people receive information, not everyone. The tendency to distribute large attachments or e-mails to everyone on a CC distribution list quickly crosses the line from efficient reminders to outright time wastage. This is often done for political reasons, in which FYI really stands for CYA (cover your assets). Updating an e-mail policy is a task bigger than any one individual can take on, yet it is the type of thing that can be tabled at an upcoming "best practices" meeting (See Chapter 14).[3]

Handle it once and keep the in-box empty. When the time comes to read your e-mail, make sure to handle it, respond to it, schedule the follow-up, and then move the letter to its appropriate folder. Even if a response is required, it makes better sense to schedule the response as a to-do and remove it from your in-box rather than leave it in there, along with 2,000 other e-mails. This is an extension of the one-you, one-calendar concept. (See Chapter 11.) The bottom line is, rather than cramming your visual workspace (your in-box)—and therefore your conscious short-term memory with passive reminders in the form of already-opened-and-awaiting-action e-mails—get them out of sight. Clear your workspace, clear your mind. Your calendar will remind you to deal with them at the appropriate time.

---

3 Check the Cool-Time website (www.cool-time.com) to download some interesting studies on the bottom-line cost of e-mail in the workplace, and new developments and options.

CHAPTER 10

E-MAIL'S A BREEZE

Perceiving just how much time is wasted when dealing with e-mail can sometimes be difficult because of its spontaneous, reactive nature. A neat analogy can be found right in your kitchen. If I told you that in a typical house, small amounts of air seep in through electrical outlets and improperly sealed doors and windows, it would probably seem insignificant. But what if I told you that added together, all those leaks are the equivalent of having a hole in the side of your house the size of a basketball? Would you want your kids eating breakfast next to a basketball-sized hole in the middle of winter? That's what e-mail has become. Collectively, it becomes a hole in the day, pouring valuable company resources—and your precious time—out into the void.

Keep the emphasis on brevity and clarity. Keep messages to one screen in length, and ask everyone you communicate with to do the same. Use bullet points rather than complete sentences. Keep paragraphs to four sentences or less.

Indicate whether a response is necessary. Some people use the subject line for this. Use the term PR (for "Please respond") as the first two characters of their subject line, as in:

[PR] Lunch Thursday?—How's 1:00P.M.?

This tells the recipient instantly that a response is necessary. If you are writing a conventional e-mail letter of three to four paragraphs, make sure also to guide your reader. Tell him what you expect as a next step in the communications chain in terms of an action or a response. Never assume that it will just happen. Tell him (tactfully) what to do.

Spell-check your subject line before sending. Spell-check might be an automatic feature for the body of a letter, but not all mail programs will check the subject line too. Poorly spelled subject lines convey a less-than-ideal image. Take a moment, just before hitting the Send button, to ensure sure your reputation for excellence continues.

Use the most time-efficient response method. Just because a message was sent to you by e-mail doesn't mean it has to be returned the same way. If it is quicker to leave a fifteen-second voicemail message to the sender, then do that. If it is quicker and clearer to wait until you meet that person face to face, then by all means, do that. Remember, e-mail may be great for confirming meeting dates or transmitting short facts, but it is not a great medium for creative synergy. The trick is to take the focus away from the actual communication tools and put the focus back on communication itself. What is the most efficient method of communicating with someone? The one that gets your message across and influences him to act without delay and without wasting your time.

Fill out the To field last. If you've ever accidentally hit the Send button before finishing the text, you know it can be a minor embarrassment. It's much easier to leave the To field blank until the very end. Not only does it eliminate any possibility of the letter being sent prematurely, you can also use it as a reminder to double-check that attachments are included.

Now...what about that pile of papers on your desk...

CHAPTER 11
THE SIXTY-SECOND WORK SPACE: A PLACE FOR EVERYTHING AND EVERYTHING IN ITS PLACE

THE LADY AND THE LIMO

A young investment adviser was hard at work trying to build his business. One of the things that bothered him the most was a "little old lady client" who lived out in the suburbs. "She has lots money," he said, "but it takes me an hour to get there, an hour to talk with her, and an hour to get back to the office. But she loves the attention and she's good for business. I just wish it didn't take up half my day!" His colleague replied, "I have someone like that too, but instead of driving out there each time, I send a limo to pick her up and take her back. It costs me $100, she gets the royal treatment, and I win back two more hours to sell more and to make more."

What does this story have to do with an organized work space? It reveals the type of strategic, time-saving approaches to problems that happen when the mind is not preoccupied with visual clutter.

Let's talk for a moment about your work space. Answer the following questions:

- Could you find any document in your work space (including in your briefcase) in less than sixty seconds?
- Could you find any document on your computer in less than sixty seconds?
- Do you like the current state of tidiness or clutter? Does it make you feel good?

Your work space, obviously, is where work gets done. It is an extension of your true working self, your mind and body. Few people have ever said, "I wish my desk was messier—it feels too barren and stark." But many have said, "I just don't have the time to tidy all this up." Or they've said, "I have tried tidying up in the past, but the mess always comes back." Or the ultimate: "I have a system. I know where everything is."

YOUR WORK SPACE IS A TOOL, NOT A TOOLBOX

A well-tuned car responds better. Sharpened pencils write better. A clear work space enables you to think better. It is hard to face the effort of tidying, especially if it has never been done before; similarly, it's a drag having to pull off the highway to get gas. But small, consistent efforts yield great results. If you start to view your work space—the desk, the computer, and the area that is your cubicle or office—as a conduit for your creativity and personal progress, you can start to condition yourself to appreciate the merits of ongoing order.

FOUND IN SIXTY SECONDS

Being able to locate any particular document in less than a minute is a necessity. The precious minutes of our lives should never be spent looking, searching, or shuffling through piles, trying to remember where something was last seen. There is tangible value in putting things away rather than pushing them aside.

There are two key components here:

- an efficient filing system
- using it regularly

Keep every project unique. Each project, client, file, or undertaking that you are working on is unique. Even if it's one of a sequence of projects for the same client, each has a particular identity, such as a file name or number, so that all correspondence, documents, files, and notes can be attributed to and stored under that number.

Whether you identify each by a name or a number is up to you, providing that the system is unmistakable. If files are filed alphabetically by name, then they'll be easy to find. If you use a numbering system, all you'll need is an index, preferably as a searchable document on your computer, in which a search for "ABC Company" will yield the correct file number, just like it does in the library.

When you use the exact same system of unique names or numbers on your PC, it will make it easier to store electronic documents within the appropriate subfolders, and the same for incoming e-mail into mail subfolders. You will have the Holy Trinity of filing:

- hard-copy files
- computer files
- e-mail files

FOLLOW-THROUGH

In golf, the swing isn't complete until the follow-through happens. Stopping the club an inch after you drive the ball would be dangerous and painful. Similarly, in the world of project management, a project doesn't end once the deliverable has been shipped. As we saw in Chapter 3, the closure phase is there to ensure that the final activities happen, even when the team is under pressure to begin the next project. Within the creative landscape of the sixty-second work space, follow-through means putting away, not putting aside. Thirty seconds spent refiling represents the closure phase of that particular mini-project. In short, when you have finished Task A and *before* you start Task B:

- documents go back into file folders
- file folders go back into filing cabinets
- computer files go back into subfolders specific to this job
- e-mails are moved from the in-box to a subfolder specific to this job

ONE YOU, ONE CALENDAR

Since there is only one of you, it makes sense that there should be only one calendar to record your actions. A human can never be in two places at once, and cannot give complete attention to more than one thing at a time. It's healthy and energizing when all activities, contacts, files, reminders, and histories remain findable within one system, not spread across many systems.

The flotsam and jetsam: Every day you will amass an unruly collection of small pieces of paper with information on them. Some, such as receipts, need to go into a file as soon as you arrive back at your desk. But the ones with information on them—business cards and sticky notes—tend to stick around, getting jammed into purses and wallets or piled on the corner of the desk since they also have important information on them. Piling up stuff for fear of losing it is the nemesis of the sixty-second work space. But just as with e-mail in your in-box, the best solution is to pull the information off the paper, put it into the system, and file the original, all as part of the follow-through of the trip or meeting just held. Do it now, before anything else.

- *Business cards:* Enter the person's particulars into your address book or contact software, and file the card away. Make a note as to what follow-up this contact needs—a reminder call six months from now, or delivery of a document that you've just promised?
- *Yellow sticky notes:* Enter the information as an appointment or to-do into your agenda, then throw away the sticky note. As useful as they are as portable notepads, the eyes quickly become used to seeing them. It's called change blindness and it's related—in the opposite way—to our compulsion to answer new e-mail, which is discussed in Chapter 2. The nervous system reacts to changes in a landscape, but becomes blind to things that don't change. Thus, a reminder to renew your driver's license

could sit, stuck to the side of your computer screen, for six months on a sticky note, and yet you'll still forget to do it.

- *Bills:* Here's a great one. You get a bill in the mail. You don't want to pay it today, but you don't want to forget about it either, so you leave it with others in an unruly pile nearby. Instead, why not note the amount and its due date into your agenda (allowing, of course, enough time for the payment to arrive by mail or Internet) and then file the bill away? That way, the information about the bill becomes a scheduled appointment on your calendar, and the mess is eliminated.

Choose a tool that's right for you. The tool for keeping track of your time should fit your mindset. If you like software, there are many great time and contact management applications available, sometimes referred to as personal information management, or PIM. If a nice book or binder is more your style, that's equally great. Hand-held PDAs are also up to the job.

Many people have, at some time or another, on someone else's advice, rushed out to purchase a brand new "time management solution" only to have it languish, unused or underused, on a corner of the desk. These people then blame themselves for not being good at organization. "If I can't use this scheduling system," they reason, "there must be something wrong with me." It's a prime source of frustration.

Your system, in order for it to work within your parameters, must be something you're comfortable with, so look for a tool that matches your taste.

Ensure that it's updated regularly. The control phase in project management exists because "things" happen. Our best-laid plans will always be affected by new developments and crises. That's why the I-Beam Agenda concept called "inventory," and its related applications such as opportunity time are so useful. With an easy-to-use calendar, and the comfort of knowing that regular, on-the-fly updates are a necessary part of sound project management and not obsessive behavior, life will be much easier and thinking a whole lot clearer.

Make a backup. One of the greatest time wasters of all, and one of the easiest to prevent, is the loss of your calendar and contact list. Do yourself a huge favor right now and schedule in a recurring reminder to back up your information. If you use software for scheduling, you can back up the files to be stored off-site. Print out a copy of your calendar and contact list at least twice a year. If you use a paper-based system, have photocopies made. If you use a PDA, ensure that the data is synchronized to a PC. It comes down to the "pay me now or pay me later" rule—the time spent backing up this data in advance is far less than the time that would be lost in trying to reconstruct your system after damage or theft has robbed you of such a crucial part of your professional life.

Make sure it covers all the bases. Whatever system—paper or electronic—that you choose, it should be able to do these things for you:

- Keep track of your appointments.
- Keep a clear list of your contacts.
- Allow you to see your to-do list and I-Beam Agenda.
- Ensure that incompleted to-do's are visible the next day.
- Present a history of your past activities.
- Present an event-by-event history of your clients, projects, and tasks.
- Remind you of recurring activities, including birthdays and anniversaries.
- Make conflicting appointments and upcoming deadlines easy to identify.
- Count down toward deadlines.
- Remind you to schedule follow-ups and follow-throughs.
- Provide for easy rescheduling.
- Provide for easy backup and remind you to do so regularly.

WHAT'S SO WRONG WITH A SYSTEM IN YOUR HEAD?

Some people pride themselves for using a system that's "entirely up here," with no need for a calendar or Daytimer. But what other great achievements could these people be capable of if their mental gifts were freed up for more challenging tasks rather than routine work? As mentioned in Chapter 4, short-term memory is not the birthplace of true achievement.

- *Making it real:* In addition to the purely practical benefits of being able to see and prioritize your appointments and to-do's, there is the psychological aspect, which states that a written, printed calendar makes tasks, goals, and deadlines more real. To believe something, we must be able to see it. It has to be committed to paper or screen. Plans that exist solely in the mind are still achievable, but their boundaries become soft. It is much easier to lose control over a scheduled activity, to make it vulnerable to distraction and delay, when its description and time line are visible only in your mind.

- *Changing on the fly:* Furthermore, when plans are written down, it is much easier to make the necessary modifications as situations force change upon you. Your flexible project plan allows for changes, while not allowing you to lose sight of those tasks that you have deemed most important.

- *Accuracy of decision:* Day plans that are committed to paper or screen help you to avoid spur-of-the-moment decisions and seat-of-the-pants reaction by putting all actions and activities into perspective. They help keep everything relative when things go smoothly, and can be a savior in times of panic.

- *Negotiation:* A visible plan is a strong negotiation tool when defending your time against people who want more of it. When they are able to see what you see, you give yourself a stronger bargaining position and a foundation for an "intelligent push-back" with managers, colleagues, and clients.

TWENTY-FIRST-CENTURY SHORTHAND

The sixty-second work space is about clarity in the physical world leading to clarity in the mental world. Another area where this has great impact is in the effort-free entry of the written word into the computer. The first of these is something you already have access to but might not use to its fullest potential:

AutoCorrect: Back in the days before personal computers and voice recognition, professional stenographers used shorthand to take notes, using a system of symbols to represent longer blocks of text. Court reporters and stenographers still use shorthand to transcribe the testimony in a courtroom.

CHAPTER 11

In Microsoft Word there is a feature called AutoCorrect (Quick-Correct in WordPerfect) that allows the rest of us to speed up the keyboarding process somewhat by using simple initials like "ap" to expand into longer terms such as "Accounts Payable" Though AutoCorrect was designed initially as a reactive tool, one that would discreetly correct improperly spelled words as you type, it is far more useful as a proactive shorthand typing tool that can actually enter many lines of text at a time. With practice and word association—another example of something the mind can do when not encumbered by visual clutter or keeping track of appointments—it is possible to memorize hundreds of entries, which will literally double or triple your keyboarding speed.[1]

Voice-recognition software: VR software transcribes dictated text into the PC, and qualifies as a Cool Time tool on two fronts. First, it is a superb replacement for typing. If your keyboarding skills are less than fluid, much time can be wasted while your fingers struggle to keep up with your thoughts. VR, however, receives and processes text at the speed of standard speech, allowing a document to be created and edited much more quickly and efficiently.

VR offers a second time management advantage through its ergonomics. By removing the need for a keyboard, the body and mind become free to move and relax. You can "write" while pacing the floor, looking up at the ceiling, gazing out through the window, or even riding an exercise bike. Your arms and shoulders need no longer be locked in the keyboard position. Your spine and muscles are free to move and stretch. Similarly, the conscious and subconscious areas of your mind are released from overconcentration, and your eyes no longer need to stare incessantly at the screen. This reduces fatigue, muscle stiffness, and the risk of longer-term repetitive stress injuries. Even if you are a swift typist, voice recognition encourages a unique creative freedom for any type of writing by liberating the rest of the body.

VR does require an initial investment of an hour or so to build a preliminary voice file, during which the software gets used to the particular timber and pace of your speech, as well as the desired volume.

---

1 If you've never used AutoCorrect or QuickCorrect before, a how-to guide is available at the Cool-Time website at www.cool-time.com.

(A quiet dictation style, spoken into a headset mike, allows VR to be used even when working in close proximity to other people.) But this investment, like so many other Cool Time techniques, pays off quickly through increased productivity, efficiency, and satisfaction. In this case, the software continues to learn, taking note of your speech patterns and building a more personalized, accurate profile as you work. Basically, the more you use it, the better it becomes and, in turn, the better you become.

And it's not just for writing novels. For example, it becomes quite a pleasure to dictate three, four, or more e-mail responses into a single temporary VR document, using the mouse only at the end to cut and paste the respective messages into separate e-mail letters.[2]

THE PERSONAL DIGITAL ASSISTANT (PDA)

The PDA is mentioned earlier as an option for maintaining a calendar and contact management. It also offers a great deal more, since its processing power and ruggedness allow the use of mainstream applications such as Microsoft Word and Excel, not to mention phone and e-mail in some cases.

This means that productivity can be achieved away from the normal workplace. A coffee shop often provides an excellent getaway to get focused keystone work done with no drop-in visitors. It means that e-mails can be read and dealt with without having to drive back to the office, and even train or plane delays cannot get in the way of productivity. (Of course, such ubiquitous access to work has a dark side in terms of addiction and workaholism, which we'll cover in Chapter 15.)

CHECKLISTS

Have you ever found yourself traveling to an appointment or to the office when you suddenly realize you've left something behind? Or you think to yourself, "Did I remember to lock the door?" Or just as you're handing a product to a client or a large document to the copy shop clerk, you're not quite sure if that crucial section was included in time? Immediately

---

2 VR brands and recommendations are available at the Cool-Time website at www.cool-time.com.

the bottom drops out of your world and your mind and body go into urgency mode as you work to figure out how best to resolve a situation that has moved beyond your control. As you try to plan your next course of action, your stress level rises, and as this happens the very parts of your mind best suited for resolving this crisis get pushed aside.

Although our day-in and day-out activities become habitual after a while, it's easy to become distracted just long enough to let one item fall through the net. Similarly, repetition begets drudgery. Our natural tendency toward rhythm increases the odds that a critical item will be overlooked, or that you will see what you expect to see, not what is actually there.

You can turn this weakness into a strength by using checklists for anything that has a series of steps—for packing, traveling, preparing for a meeting, scheduling a project—anything in which a predictable or required sequence can be planned for and then activated.

- Checklists help ensure that everything necessary for successful project completion is accounted for.
- Checklists eliminate the need to rely on short-term and long-term memory whose talents, as we have seen, lie in things other than photographic recall of lists.
- By freeing short-term memory from the drudgery of a set sequence, mental energy is given over to more creative, strategic, profitable tasks.
- Checklists ensure consistency of action and quality.
- Consistency opens the door to delegation by turning expertise into modular, transferable components. Once a task is delegated, our own energies and expertise can be applied concurrently to a more profitable or valuable task.
- Checklists help eliminate the stress or guilt that happens when something crucial is forgotten.
- They can be edited and refined after each event as part of the process of continual improvement, making them even more useful as time goes by.

Think about all the situations in which a checklist could benefit you:

- When you leave for work in the morning, how many items (car keys, sunglasses, cellphone, etc.) do you need to have with you—items that can be easily forgotten? How many times have you had to run around looking for the car keys or your sunglasses because they're nowhere to be found?
- Also, when leaving for work in the morning, how many things about your outward appearance need to be checked, such as hair, clothing, zippers, jewelry, etc.—things that could be easily overlooked if you are in a hurry?
- At work, whether you're visiting a new client, going for an interview, giving a presentation, or meeting someone for lunch, there are numerous questions that need to be answered to ensure that you arrive in Cool Time, such as:

  - What is the destination address?
  - What is the nearest cross street?
  - Is parking available? If so, where?
  - What is the contact's name?
  - What is the contact's phone number?
  - Is there an alternate contact?
  - What is the alternate's phone number?
  - Are there prior security or access arrangements to be made?
  - Have I called to confirm the appointment two days prior?
  - How can the contact reach me if there is an emergency or change of plan?
  - Have I packed everything I need to take?

And what about school-age kids? How much easier would it be to get everyone to the school bus if they had all they needed?

It's worth investing the time to create checklists, and to always have them nearby. They play a major part in establishing positive image and great rapport by ensuring that your creative mind is assigned to creative things, not procedural ones.

This is part of the reason for the I-Beam Base—to ask yourself "What happened today that I could improve upon? Is there a sequence that I could factor in, together with a project plan, to ensure that I arrive on time and totally together?"

CHARISMA—THE ESSENCE OF COOL

Think for a moment of a famous person you admire—maybe a leader like Martin Luther King or Nelson Mandela, perhaps a performer or a business leader. If you ask yourself to identify what you admire about this person, your answers might include looks, mannerisms, sense of self, confidence, vision, or credibility. It can usually come down to one word: charisma. Celebrities make it their business to always appear in control, living on a plane of achievement far above the ordinary person. It's an ideal, the end result of money, power, and influence. However, it's not exclusive to them. Cool Time techniques such as project planning and, yes, even the humble checklist, help to restore control and vision into the lives of anyone who chooses to adopt them. It's a way to achieve the type of charisma that our heroes have.

RECORD EVERYTHING

The human mind is a remarkable instrument with a phenomenal capacity for long-term memory and creative thought. But often the smaller, temporary items, those that exist solely in short-term memory, do not get the chance to stick. It has been proven that short-term memory can manage a maximum of about seven items at a time. Therefore, if you have more than seven tasks to perform today, or seven items to buy at a store, you will most likely forget a few unless you write them down.

The strongest memory is weaker than the palest ink, so make notes. This is an expression with great significance. Making notes is never wrong, whether it's during a meeting, an interview, or immediately afterwards. Whenever you find yourself trying to remember something,

something that you had the opportunity to write down earlier, you lose opportunity and time.

- *Voice recorders:* Voice recorders are inexpensive hand-held devices. Some cellphones and PDAs have voice recording built in, and pretty much everyone has voicemail or a telephone answering machine. Thus, wherever you are in the world, you have access to a quick note-taking, fact-grabbing tool to capture your thoughts, ideas, and lists and hold them until you're ready for them.
- *A phone log:* A phone log stores the details of each of your phone calls. Just a simple document in Microsoft Word or WordPerfect will do, in which each entry includes the caller, date, and time of day. Not only does this help keep track of the large number of calls you handle, if you wish to review every time that Mary Jones called you or was called by you, a simple Find search from the Edit menu will locate your entire chronological relationship with her.
- *A project log:* Similar to a phone log, a project log focuses on a single project or client. And the extra work is minimal—you simply copy and paste all of the phone log entries pertaining to the people involved in the project into your project log, along with notes on meetings, activities, and developments, so that they're together in one file ready for review.
- *Leveraging your creativity:* Every day, people come up with brilliant thoughts and ideas that would pay off in marvelous ways for them. And all too often these thoughts disappear on the breeze because their short-term memories are already too full.

How beneficial it would be, then, to note down new activities and thoughts the moment you think of them—into a PDA, a voice recorder, or onto a piece of paper—to create opportunity for new thoughts and ideas to arrive.

THE KNOWLEDGE BASE

In addition to remembering names and events, we are expected to retain and use all the knowledge we acquire throughout our lives. Some professions require continuing education to be part of the job, and every year millions of people take courses or training sessions to further their knowledge and expertise. There are also books and e-mail newsletters to read, and TV shows to watch. The problem is, there's so much information out there that it's easy to forget much of what is taught. It's the old 80/20 rule again. Twenty percent of what you take in will be retained as knowledge and remain accessible. The rest lurks around there somewhere, but removes itself from the grasp of short-term memory to the point that it becomes useless. But remember, the Cool Time philosophy is about using your time for maximum effectiveness, allowing nothing to fall into the cracks—not names, not events, and especially not knowledge—and the Cool Time sixty-second work space is about being able to recall all that in under a minute. That is why you need to create a knowledge base.

A knowledge base is your personal collection of facts and points, garnered from all the books, newsletters, articles, and digests that cross your path, all of it categorized and quickly accessible. Usually in any publication or essay there are just a couple of "aha moments," those unique points around which the article is based, and these are what go into your knowledge base.

The most useful format for a knowledge base is a single document in Microsoft Word or WordPerfect, an e-document. Since e-documents can run into the hundreds of pages, there's plenty of room for it to grow with you. Your knowledge base can have as many pages in it as necessary, each focusing on a different area of knowledge. Then, as you see a key point in an article, you can open up your knowledge base and enter the quote and its source onto the appropriate page.[3]

- By assigning a "bookmark" to each page/chapter head within the knowledge base, you can create a hyperlinked table of contents on the first page, so that if you wish to paste a new quote into your chapter on "Leadership," you simply click on "Leadership" within the table of contents and it takes you directly there.

---

3 A guide on how to set up your own knowledge base, including creating "bookmarks" and other techniques, is available in The *Cool-Time Action Plan Workbook*, at www.cool-time.com.

- If the quote you include has further details accessible at a website, or you wish to include the e-mail address of the author, both of these can be entered as part of the article to allow instant access to further useful information.
- Your knowledge base can travel with you on a PDA, a CD, or a floppy disk, so that you're never far from its rich collection of knowledge.
- A knowledge base is best updated during the I-Beam Base period at the end of the day. Remember, this is a time set aside for continual improvement, which is what the knowledge base offers. As your day proceeds, set aside any articles of interest, highlight the best parts, copy and paste text from on-line articles and e-mails along with their URLs, and leave them all for processing at the end of the day.
- The best way to capitalize on the knowledge base would be to review one page or one chapter a day, every day, perhaps even setting up a daily reminder in your daytimer or PIM to make sure you do it.

People often respond to the knowledge base concept by saying, "I haven't got the time or discipline to set that up, maintain it, and read it." Well, if something is important enough to you, you will find the time. In this case, think about its value. Knowledge is power. Every fact, concept, or memory that escapes you is opportunity lost. Every fact that can be quickly retained and used is another arrow in your quiver. A versatile knowledge base is a formidable ally.

CHAPTER 12
WORK–LIFE BALANCE:
THE CIRCULAR ENGINE

Time management success is by no means limited to business hours. There is a twenty-four-hour cycle to be observed, one of the many rhythms of the human metabolism, which, like a wheel, obtains perfection and balance by rotating and moving forward.

There are three time zones through which we pass on any given workday that correspond to work, sleep, and personal time.

Work obviously represents the time we spend at work, or school, doing the things we are paid or expected to do. *Sleep* represents the time we spend asleep. *Personal* represents the time we spend doing anything else that is neither work nor sleep—the fun, the mundane, and the necessary.

There are only three sections on this wheel, though the components that make up our personal time may be divided throughout the day to reflect morning activities, noon activities, and after-work activities.

The goal is to keep the wheel in balance and in motion, which is not always easy. If you accept the

North American workday as ranging between eight and twelve hours, with the average adult sleep period between five and eight hours, this leaves us just a few extra hours to get everything else done, including commuting, lunch, groceries, hobbies, and leisure. The pressures of work and school, as well as the ever-rising bar of our own expectations, add more hours to the work side, like this:

The North American work ethic encourages overwork, sometimes using the number of hours worked as the main index of busyness. Though we might derive a temporary sense of achievement from such efforts, we do so at a great price, for the human metabolism is a strict creditor.

SLEEP: THE METABOLIC BODY SHOP

Did you know that the latest studies show that the average North American adult requires around nine hours of sleep a night? When was the last time you got that much sleep on a weeknight? Most people get six, seven, or maybe eight. That's why there are coffee shops on every corner. We have grown to accept caffeine as the bandage for a fractured circadian rhythm.

But stimulants alleviate the symptoms only temporarily. Sleep deficiency is still sleep deficiency. When someone who really needs eight hours of sleep gets only six on Sunday night, Monday starts with a sleep debt of two hours. If the same thing happens on Monday night, then the sleep debt on Tuesday becomes four hours. As the week wears on, the effects of ongoing sleep deficit compound themselves, which affects a lot of things in a bad way.

Sleep might seem nothing more than a period of unconsciousness, but the hours between midnight and 5:00 a.m. are actually a symphony of activity. This late-night deep-sleep period sees breathing and pulse rates drop to a very low ebb. Meanwhile, the body is hard at work replacing skin cells, repairing the minor damage of the day, reinforcing the immune system, and generally fixing itself up for its next shift. At the same time, the brain constructs elaborate "what-if" scenarios, creating fantastic and strange dreams in which our sleeping bodies exist as both observer and participant. These weird scenes, culled and mixed equally from deep, long-held memories as well as the events of the past few hours, are played out like a movie in the short-term memory area of the brain. The thoughts and ideas processed during this time are, in most cases, forgotten when we wake up, which is why all but the most vivid dreams are hard to remember. In short, the sleep period is one of rebuilding, testing, and analyzing, a nightly act of fine-tuning and adjustment that ensures optimum performance during our waking hours.

PERSONAL TIME

The personal component of the day involves everything that is neither work nor sleep—doing the laundry and buying the groceries, but also relaxing, doing physical exercise, enjoying hobbies, spending quality time—all the things we *like* to do.

When work schedules forcibly reduce the sleep and personal time blocks, the amount of time available for strengthening, rebuilding, and maintaining those very parts of us that are expected to be productive while on the job are reduced.

YOUR PERSONAL VEIN OF GOLD

Prospectors search the land, looking desperately for pay dirt, their very own vein of gold. It's hidden, under rock and mud, the debris of the everyday.

Each of us has a creative mind, capable of great ideas, pure enjoyment, and perfect balance, yet it is buried beneath the weight of distraction, the stress of the day. Here's a situation that illustrates the point.

You're having a conversation with someone in which you're discussing a particular actor in a movie you once saw. But try as you might, the actor's name eludes you. "Wait a minute," you say, "it's on the tip of my tongue." But it doesn't come. So you continue the dialogue and eventually change the subject. Two minutes later, while you're in the middle of talking about something else, it comes to you. You snap your fingers. "Now I remember," you exclaim, and the name rolls off your tongue as easy as can be.

Success came the moment you let your mind relax on the particular problem. It's like making a fist inside a glass jam jar. As long as your hand remains a fist, you will not be able to get it out of the jar. As soon as it relaxes, escape is easy. If you had continued to struggle to remember the name of the actor, the struggle would have held your mental doors tightly closed. But the moment you let go, the stress of that small situation subsided, and the answer came forth.

Exercise: The mind is more creative when the body is exercised: Personal time, especially during the evening, is needed to drain stress and tension from the body, and to allow the mind to roam free. Personal time activities can be vigorous, such as playing sports or playing with the kids, or they can be calmer, such as taking a brisk walk, gardening, or washing the car. By letting yourself, or even forcing yourself, to schedule some exercise time, you will actually enhance your at-work productivity. Ideas, inspiration, solutions to problems all blossom when you exercise. Exercise also elevates moods and enhances feelings of optimism. It wards off depression, anxiety, and other affective disorders. And even if you're in a high-stress, high-anxiety situation, a high-intensity workout of twenty minutes or more will help calm you down. Remember to always carry your voice recorder or a pen and paper to capture those great ideas!

Eating: Having proper time to digest is central to weight control: Regularly scheduled personal time allows for the enjoyment of a healthy diet at a healthy time of day. Eating at 9:00P.M. or 10:00P.M. does not give the body sufficient opportunity to digest before the sleep phase sets in, which results in improper digestion, leading to greater amounts of food energy being stored as fat.

High-quality sleep: We may not be able to get the requisite nine hours of sleep per night, but there is a lot we can do to help ensure that high-quality sleep comes on faster and lasts longer, just by letting the body's chemistry do what it wants to do. The chemicals such as melatonin, which helps facilitate sleep, are released into the bloodstream over a number of hours from mid-afternoon onward. Personal time helps ensure that these chemicals exert their proper influence, making us drowsy and ready to sleep. Working late into the night and sacrificing personal time forces the body to counteract the effects of melatonin, thus creating a chemical conflict that makes it harder to go to sleep when you eventually get to bed. And the price paid extends into the next day in the form of fatigue, headaches, and generally lower energy levels.

Breaks, an opportunity for refueling: Everyone knows what it feels like to work through lunch, or to work without a break. When opportunities for refueling and physical and mental regrouping are denied, the potential for errors, burnout, and pain increases as blood sugar levels drop and the body is forced to turn to more drastic means to sustain itself, as we'll discuss later in this chapter. In addition, the overfatigue brought on by food deprivation will further affect the sleep cycle by delaying its onset and reducing the efficiency of its stages.

Personal time helps you be your best: Success is driven by positive mental energy and positive thought. Top-notch achievers always appear competent, confident, and capable. They inspire others, and are looked to for leadership and guidance. They derive part of this luster through some sort of non-work-related personal activity to balance the stresses and demands of their work lives. By contrast, people who appear dragged-out, sleepy, and irritable seldom generate credibility or respect in the eyes of their clients and colleagues. The investment in personal time, combined with healthy diet and sleep habits, will have as much to do with your success and satisfaction as your education, wardrobe, or experience.

The prestige factor: There is a great deal of pride and panache in putting in a good day's work, then going home. Whereas at one time people looked upon the sixteen-hour-a-day workaholic as the go-getter, the company star, this is thankfully no longer the case. Face-time is still important, of course, but quality, combined with frequent communication, outdoes excessive quantity every time. If you need to stay until 10:00P.M. every night to get your work finished, what does that say about the way you run your company or your affairs? Excellence is derived from doing top-notch work in well-planned segments, rather than struggling through a continuum of never-ending tasks. Let people know that you'll always be available, but do it in a way that defends your time first. Keep in mind the essential triumvirate—a carefully planned work period cushioned by sufficient personal time, balanced by healthy sleep time.

PERSONAL TIME VS. NEGATIVE-VALUE TIME

Cost of acquisition is a well-known term in business. If it costs more, in terms of preparation, research, development, and marketing to make a product than you stand ultimately to gain in its sale, that might not be a good thing. In Cool Time the same principle applies. Given the absolute importance of having personal time in your twenty-four-hour day, there are very real consequences when you mess with it. If you choose to work through this period, be careful to not let the value of that work turn into a loss, a negative value. Here's the math:

- First, think about the perceived value of the work that you might get done during your personal time. You could say to yourself, "I'm getting two-and-a-half hours' worth of work done this evening, which has a dollar value, or an achievement value of A."
- But then think of the value of those same personal time hours in terms of family, friends, and leisure. If you were to put a price on the time you spend doing things you love or being with people you love (or both), it might have a value of B.
- If you also admit that there were some parts of the day just past in which there was wastage or distraction, where you *could have* done some of the work that you have now assigned to the evening, then the value of that lost time we'll call C.
- Finally, there's all the positive benefits of wind-down time that you're missing out on, including exercise, eating a proper meal at the proper time, and just having time for yourself. This value we'll call D.
- If the sum of $B + C + D$ is greater than A: $A - (B + C + D) < 0$, then the work attains a negative value.

You might argue that you're not staying late by choice—the work has to be done! How much of the work done during personal time could have been done during the day, or could be done tomorrow, or could have been delegated to someone else? How much are you allowing your schedule to dictate your day by not identifying top-priority tasks, by reacting to urgencies, and by not defending your productive time against intrusion? How much is your job running you? To stay in control of your schedule means reviewing and planning it realistically and regularly, to communicate with clients and to manage their expectations, and to know the value of every moment of your day. Just because there is an evening that follows the day doesn't mean it's free to be used for more work. Complete as much of the right work as you can, then go home. There will always be new mail arriving, more voicemail to return, more work left to finish, but you can do it at its appropriate time. Go home.

THE MARATHON RUNNER

Marathon runners understand the balance between work and life. Rather than running without a plan, they know how to pace themselves, thus preserving energy and ensuring they remain properly hydrated. No professional marathon runner has ever sprinted the entire twenty-six miles, and no matter how lucrative a running career may be, the true professional knows better than to run a second marathon the very next day.

People who work too hard for too long experience burnout, fatigue, and injury. Long-term illnesses resulting from unrelieved stress do nothing to advance your reputation as an achiever. Your body simply can't keep up the same level of intensity for protracted periods. Thus, investing in even small amounts of leisure on a daily basis will contribute to increased productivity and quality in the short term and the avoidance of longer-term injuries later on.

CHAPTER 12

A BLUEPRINT FOR YOUR HEALTH

You can see by now that Cool Time isn't simply about working efficiently during your working hours. It's about how you protect yourself
as you travel along the straight path of time. It's about recognizing that
your body and mind together form your singular vehicle of transit, and
that daily maintenance is not a bad idea. The suggestions in this section
all focus on helping your physical, intellectual, and emotional self be the
best it can, by providing resources and sustenance at minimal cost.

Air: If you work in a commercial building, chances are it is hermeti-
cally sealed. For the economic well-being of the building and its owners,
the air we breathe is locked inside and recirculated. Revolving doors ensure
that only a bare minimum of air is exchanged when people enter or exit
the building. When you travel by plane, you get to experience the same
situation in miniature as air is breathed in and out by the same people and
recirculated for hours on end. In both cases, in the sky and in your office,
this can lead to fatigue, headaches, and a suppression of the immune system. In extreme cases, it's a contributor to "sick building syndrome."

Can you combat this stale-air problem by opening a window? Not
in most downtown buildings, but you can at least secure a more vibrant
and healthy existence for yourself by ensuring that your day includes
those breaks we talked about above, as well as time for lunch. These are
times when you can actually get up, leave what you're doing, and go
outside. Even during the depths of winter or the extreme heat of summer, five minutes outside will help to revitalize you, ushering a badly
needed change of air into your lungs and bloodstream.

If your office or working circumstances allow, you might also want
to consider bringing in an ionizer and a small fan to ensure a flow of
revitalized air around your face. The important thing is to keep air
flowing around you. The sensation of gently moving air acts as a stimulant, keeping the mind and body alert and upbeat.

Blue-sky: The term "to blue-sky" means to stare up at the sky and to
let your mind wander. Factoring in some blue-sky time, perhaps while
you eat your lunch or while you take a break, gives your mind a chance
to also take a break. Being absorbed in a good book has the same effect.

It takes you away for a moment, and the effects are very positive. By contrast, those who read work-related material during lunch, or check voicemail on a quick break, are only getting half the benefit. The mind needs freedom, too.

Natural light: The human body thrives on natural light. It regulates our inner circadian rhythm, it stimulates us to get up in the morning, and a lack of it depresses our metabolism. It's no surprise, then, that the most coveted rooms in any building are on the outside corners. This is not simply because of the space and the view; it's light that helps us feel great, helps us feel alive. If you work where there is natural light nearby, you're very lucky. If you can open the window in your office, you're extremely lucky.

We need natural light. Many people in northern latitudes fall victim each January and February to seasonal affective disorder (SAD), a prolonged state of sadness, depression, and lethargy. It has a number of sources, including the prolonged lack of light experienced during those winter months. We need natural light to feel up to par. If you do not have access to natural light at your workspace, you now have a second reason to take a least two breaks per day (plus lunch) in which you get up, leave your desk, and go outside.

In addition, you might want to consider purchasing a full-spectrum desk lamp. These emit a healthier, more eye-pleasing illumination to help counter the flicker of computer screens and overhead fluorescent lights.

Food: Our desire for sugar and fats is a self-preservation instinct, sustained for thousands of years by the fact that we had to work a lot harder to find food of any sort while not becoming food for something else. So caloric intake and expenditure pretty much balanced out. Fat became the storehouse for future famines. Our bodies still react in the same way, only now food (for most of us) is abundant, and the highly refined sugars and flours that comprise fast-food meals require so little energy to process that it is easy for the body to convert them to fat. There's nothing else it needs them for. But darn it, donuts are tasty, so have a donut (just one). Go ahead. But try also to seek balance by having something else as well, something more substantial, more beneficial. If denying yourself a donut will make you feel deprived (and depraved), then have it and enjoy it.

Remember, though, that donuts and other sweet snacks provide only a quick sugar high, full of empty calories, which do nothing to support your metabolism over the long term. In fact, that sugar high can lead to a sugar hangover within minutes, bringing on feelings of sluggishness and fatigue.

Eating healthily does not have to be boring. More and more, food courts and restaurants provide healthy offerings that are reasonably priced and very satisfying. They sell good, light meals and snacks, just when your body needs them, providing energy for the afternoon and helping to counteract that mid-afternoon low.

Our physical desire for food, the concept and sensation that is hunger, has been carefully studied by fast-food operations. As a result, their products are often high in sugar, sodium, starch, and saturated fat, which quickly satisfy hunger pangs, but do little to fuel the body over the long term. Even colors have a great influence on appetite and our choice of what to eat. Bright reds and yellows are proven to do more to stimulate hunger than other colors. Now think of the major fast-food restaurant chains in your neighborhood. What colors are in their signs and wrappers? Even the local pizzeria will likely have red-checkered tablecloths. It works!

Successful defense and use of time can happen only on a full stomach. After all, food is fuel. You can't manage your time without managing your physical self. Most people would never consider pouring a cupful of sugar into their car's gas tank, but they don't think anything of doing the same to themselves.

Skipping meals: Try not to skip meals either. The frequency of your food intake has major implications on all aspects of your life. Breakfast, as you know, is the most important meal of the day. Your body, starving after ten hours or more of not eating, needs carbohydrates, proteins, vitamins, and natural sugars to carry you through until the next refueling period at lunch. People who skip breakfast or lunch because they don't have enough time to eat or, worse, because they think they can lose weight this way, are doing themselves harm on both counts. If they skip meals because of time constraints, they are condemning themselves to a full day of reduced energy and reduced attention span. When food is eaten in moderate amounts throughout the day, it results in greater stamina, attention, and good feeling. Those who skip meals as part of a weight-loss plan are inadvertently tricking their own bodies into think-ing that there is a famine, and the body will shift into survival mode and start to break down muscle fiber, which can be metabolized more easily than fat. This means that the next time you eat, your body will store any extra energy in case of another famine, and turn it into fat. So skipping meals can be an effective weight-gain plan, not a weight-loss plan.

If you're worried about overeating, try having some low-fat yogurt twenty minutes before your main meal. The protein in the yogurt will satisfy those feelings of hunger, allowing you to eat your lunch more calmly and selectively.[1]

In both of the above cases, the solution is to aim for regular in-take of reasonable foods. Have breakfast. Enjoy a mid-morning snack followed by lunch, a mid-afternoon snack, and then dinner. It's not impossible. Apples, cheese, fruits, pita bread, and nuts are healthy products that need little preparation, can sit in your desk or on the back seat of your car, and are easily available at the supermarket. Five small meals a day will go much further in terms of stamina, ability, and weight control; but like so many other points in this book, adopt-ing such a regime would seem culturally strange, which is why so few people do it.

SUPPER TIME

The supper hour known in North America was actually devised as a method of timing shifts coming home from factories. Though "sup-per" has always been considered the main meal in many cultures, scheduling it so late in the day is relatively modern. In earlier times, people ate four or five smaller meals throughout the day. It was only the economic concerns of the factory owners of Victorian England, and later the rest of the industrialized world, that forced us to eat a disproportionately large amount of food so close to bedtime.

---

1 This fact, as well as many other extremely useful health and diet-related tips, can be found in Dr. Robert Arnot's book, *The Biology of Success*, and Rick Gallop's *The G.I. Diet*, both of which are highlighted on the Cool-Time website, www.cool-time.com.

STRATEGIC VACATION PLANNING

Most people look forward to their vacation, and rightly so. This is supposed to be the time of relaxation and recharging. It's essential for maintaining balance. Your vacation should be treated as one of the most important parts of your job because that's just what it is. It needs to be defended. This means taking time to plan the vacation period carefully to help ensure a smooth, stress-free departure and a smooth, stress-free return.

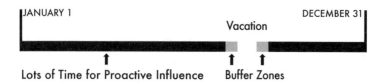

Plan ahead to avoid the pre-vacation crunch. The last few days at the office before a vacation can be the most stressful of all as it seems all the work that you would have had to do if you weren't going on vacation immediately becomes a top priority and absolutely must get finished before your departure.

This is a completely avoidable situation, since vacations rarely come as a surprise. Most vacation times are reserved many months in advance to ensure that everybody will not take off at the same time. Therefore, if you start planning your departure many months before the actual date, you should be able to influence the time lines of projects, meetings, and other office events that the vacation conflicts with.

It's essential to draw a protective barrier around the period of your vacation, including the ten business days leading up to it and the ten immediately following it. Make sure those days before your vacation are carefully planned, so that you are able to either hand off responsibilities to others or wrap up parts of a project. The days preceding a vacation should not be business as usual for you. If you try to keep working on your normal tasks at your normal pace on these days, you will generate more stress and overwork than the holiday could possibly alleviate. Before going on vacation you should:

- Draw up a list of colleagues who can be counted on to perform small tasks on your behalf, such as returning a call to a key client, or ensuring delivery of a package on the first Monday of your holiday.
- Set up instructions on your outgoing voicemail message and on your e-mail auto-reply to let everyone know you'll be unavailable. Ask them to call back after a certain date rather than leave a message, and make this a date that is definitely not your first day back in the office.
- Avoid leaving a contact number at your vacation place for everyone's knowledge. If your position is such that you must be reachable for the highest-level emergency, leave your number with someone you trust.

Rest and relaxation are of the utmost importance. Even if you thrive on daily contact, the restorative properties of a properly prepared vacation will enhance your working abilities on your return.

- *Keep your priorities in view.* Not all work will be finished by the time your holiday starts. Some things can wait or can be delegated. And you know what? The company will survive without you, at least for a couple of weeks. Avoid taking on additional projects during this time, since these activities will only cloud the enjoyment of your holiday. Remind people that you will soon be back, and that life will go on.
- *Give your phone a holiday, too.* Your cellphone deserves a break as well. I recommend you keep it with you during holidays, but only for personal security or to keep in touch with family members. Let the cellphone itself be a reminder of what your vacation stands for—after all, when its batteries run down, you have no choice but to give them time to recharge. Shouldn't you do yourself the same favor?
- *Leave an hour early on the last day before your vacation.* This is pure self-indulgence, and it feels absolutely great, which in itself goes a long way toward establishing balance in your life and getting your vacation off on the right foot. Enjoy the freedom of that stolen hour. Definitely avoid working late on your holiday eve. This robs you and your family of the good feeling that a holiday should bring. It is unfair and completely avoidable. Take off. Go and have a great time.

- *Plan your return before you leave.* Though most people don't want to even think about their return to work as they start their holiday, a smooth return will help to ease the stress of re-entering the rat race. The day of your return should not include meetings. It should be a transition day, in which much of the time is given over to catching up on the events that happened during your absence. Your keystone time for that day should consist of focusing on returning calls, up-dating your I-Beam Agenda, and getting back up to speed.

  Why is this so important? Because too many people simply return to the office and hit the ground running, trying to imme-diately regain the pace they were at when they left. They return straight away to the stress levels and pressures that they left behind, losing much of the therapeutic benefits that they may have gained from their vacation. Remember, your vacation is a time for relax-ation and rebuilding. It is part of your job. You benefit, your family benefits, and your company benefits. Ease your way back into the momentum of work, just like a runner warming up before a mara-thon, and you will be better prepared to handle it. And, of course, start planning your next vacation immediately!

- *Consider spending part of your vacation at home.* A two-week vacation in the Caribbean sounds great, but a ten-day island vacation, bracket-ed by four days at home, may be even more relaxing. Spending some time at home while everyone at the office thinks you're away gives you the chance to get a few things done, to enjoy a rare respite of quiet in the house, to catch up on a few overdue tasks, and put your mind at rest. A couple of days at home before you depart for your holiday trip, followed by a couple of days after, also allows you to prepare for your trip and travel to the airport in Cool Time without stress, hurry, or forgetting anything.

The same applies to your return. This is especially important if you plan to travel during traditional holiday periods such as Thanksgiving and Christmas when travel routes are packed. The secret is to have a comfortable holiday and not let anyone know you're back until your second day back at the office. Plan your vacation as you would plan any other project. Make room for contingencies and delegate authority to others. Work diligently to ensure that your return to work is as stress-free as your vacation itself.

CHAPTER 13
COOL TIME: PERFECTION
THROUGH PRECISION

TRAVELING IN COOL TIME

Traveling in Cool Time means that as you head to an appointment, you do so at a normal pace. Having allowed yourself sufficient and realistic travel time, you walk comfortably and drive more safely. It allows you to enjoy a few moments of mental rest between appointments, to move at a pace that guarantees punctuality, yet that also allows your mind the time and opportunity to focus on the upcoming activity and shape its outcome.

Cool Time allows you to stay physically cool, since frustration can be a powerful internal source of heat. A physically cool self means neat, clean clothes. It means a confident, dry handshake, clear eye contact, and a friendly face. Cool Time allows you time to control your appearance.

Wherever you travel and whomever you meet, your arrival sets the tone permanently for the relationship in the future. If you are meeting someone for the first time, you will have just that one chance to make a first impression. Traveling in Cool Time means adding a few minutes to your schedule to ensure that you present the best possible image to your audience. In can make all the difference in the world.

CHAPTER 13

A Cool-Time Example

Suppose you have a meeting scheduled for 2:00P.M. In Cool Time, you focus on arriving at 1:50. When people make plans with the actual meeting time as their goal, they increase greatly the chances of being late because they aim too close. As the expression goes, "If you plan to be on time, you plan to be late."

Make a realistic calculation of the time you will need to get from your workplace to the meeting by 1:50P.M. Is it a five-minute walk? A cross-town drive? Are there slow elevators or security check-ins to factor in? Accept these constraints, don't wish them away or gamble that you'll hit every green light on your way to the meeting. Cool Time is about planning without misconception, traveling without rushing, and includes safe, sane driving and stress-free movement.

Cool Time is about making these elements real by entering them into the I-Beam Agenda with pragmatic reality. Though the face-to-face component of the meeting starts at 2:00P.M., the activity called "the Meeting" actually begins the moment you pull together the required materials, get up from your desk, and start traveling.

And if the phone rings as you get up to leave, *think before answering*. This is precisely how so many people make themselves late. Stay cool and decide before answering if the caller is one of your top-priority people, or whether your clear, proactive voicemail greeting can take care of their needs for the moment. Cool Time avoids the temptations of Answerholism. Unless the call is of top-level urgency, consider yourself officially already gone—already in the meeting. After all, if the caller had called a minute later, you would already be on your way, and voicemail would have taken over anyway.

Though the actual meeting is scheduled from 2:00P.M. until 3:00P.M., you've calculated, as part of your morning I-Beam Review, that Cool Time travel will require forty-five minutes, including getting up from your desk, waiting for the elevator, getting to your car, and getting through city traffic to the highway. As well, you'll need a few minutes after the meeting for follow-up and summarizing (closure). Therefore, the meeting really lasts from 1:15P.M. to 3:15P.M. That's what you tell yourself and those around you. The meeting is from 1:15 P.M. to 3:15 P. M. because it is.

With Cool Time you will stride into your meeting exactly on time, avoiding the many negative repercussions of lateness. Lateness is not a great career advancement tool. It's disruptive, embarrassing, and professionally damaging to have to enter a closed-door meeting, find a chair, unpack, and collect yourself under the gaze of all others present. It is equally difficult to have to explain to a client why you are late for a planned and confirmed one-on-one meeting.

But arriving early doesn't mean you have to appear until precisely the right moment. Let's say you arrive at a meeting a full half-hour early due to clear roads. Well, now, that's the time you can use to take those calls that came in just as you were leaving. You're parked, you're in sight of the building or meeting room, you're early, and the people you're meeting don't know you're here yet. Perfect! You've got some keystone time, private and undisturbed, to make a few phone calls or do some work. With a cellphone, a PDA, and a briefcase, even a pen, paper, and some coins, downtime becomes productive time. All you've done is reversed the order—travel first, then take the calls.

Maybe you could spend the bonus time relaxing—imagine that! Enjoy a few minutes of sunshine, read a newspaper, or grab a coffee. A fifteen-minute, blue-sky mini-vacation is a healthy, productive use of your time—it really is. Then, when you're ready, make your appearance five minutes before the arranged meeting time, exactly as planned. You will soon have people saying, "You know, I can set my watch by you— you're always on time," which is an attribute that parlays into success very quickly in our time-conscious world.

COOL TIME IN THE MORNING: GETTING UP

Most people hate getting up in the morning, and with good reason. The warmth, the comfort, the protection afforded by our beds is unmatched. It is a place where we feel most secure, even though we are physically most vulnerable. Have you noticed that when you travel, whether for business or pleasure, your entire perspective about the trip changes when you first open the hotel room door and survey your new bed for the first time? This strange place is your temporary home, your refuge in a strange land. In our minds, all of our physical journeys—to the office and back, grocery shopping, or traveling on vacation—can be drawn on a map as lines radiating from our pillow, the epicenter of our existence. Wherever you go, in the back of your mind you will always have a plan of how to return to your pillow by the end of the day.

Getting up, then, is the first of a number of personal sacrifices and concessions that we have to make every day. It is a tormenting separation from the bliss and warmth of sleep. To prolong the comfort as much as possible, many people will spend the least amount of time necessary on dressing, preparing, and traveling to work. And if they think of it, they might even grab something to eat on their way out the door.

But getting up in the morning is one of the few things over which we as individuals have a lot of control, since there are no appointments that precede it. It's the first event of the day. It is an exercise in mental determination—mind over mattress.

Get a better alarm clock. If you decide to buy one thing on the strength of reading this book, this should be it: an alarm clock that doesn't alarm, but wakes gently, one that gradually raises its volume over the course of twenty minutes; one that has a small column of lights that illuminate gradually, so that the stimulation to wake up synchronizes better with your sleep cycle.[1] By contrast, an alarm clock that goes off with a buzzer or a bell in your ear is only one step removed from a bucket of ice water being poured over you. Given the limited hours of sleep we have available, being ripped from REM sleep is a great cause of headaches at least, and heart attacks at worst. Mondays are big days for heart attacks in North America, as people get shocked out of the semi-relaxation of the weekend, and are forced to recall all of the stresses they left behind on Friday.

Hit the light switch, not the snooze bar. Use light right away to capitalize on your circadian rhythm. Light stimulates the brain, which

---

1 A listing of recommended alarm clock brands and suppliers is available at the Cool-Time website at www.cool-time.com.

releases stimulant chemicals into the bloodstream. Turn on your bedside light as soon as the alarm rings and sit up. If you have a partner who gets to go on sleeping, use a flashlight. Nobody cares what you look like at that time of the morning. They're either still asleep, or they'll look the same as you. Light and color before your eyes will work at eliminating sleepiness from the inside even before your first coffee.

Make getting up worth it. Think for a moment back to the great events in your life—Christmases, holidays, and birthdays during your childhood; the first day of school; the first snowy morning; your wedding day; or the first day of a new job. You might recall that getting up on those days was a lot easier than usual. There were big things afoot, things that snapped your mind into action and pulled you up to start the big day ahead.

Now, how can we give that same luster of excitement to every day? The benefits of being up must outweigh the benefits of being in bed. Your initial reflex during that the first moment of a new day, when the alarm shatters the peace of early morning, must be one of action, not reaction. Immediately start to think to yourself, *There is more to be gained from getting up now than from staying in bed*, because when you believe that, it will turn out to be true. Start thinking about things—activities, ideas, plans for the day. Get your mind moving and your body will follow.

Every day has the potential to move your life forward in the direction you wish. It may not be easy at first, but everyone can find something special to look forward to in every single day to use as motivation for getting up.

- If you have a big event scheduled for today, a positive achievement that you know you can complete, then remember it! Picture it. Tell yourself that the road to that achievement starts right now.
- If you have a less positive event scheduled for today, something you dread, something that you'd rather not face, then focus on its completion. Look forward to getting it over with. Take the bull by the horns and tell yourself that by getting up now, you will be taking the first step toward completing and eliminating this unpleasant task, after which better things, or healing, can start.

- If your upcoming day and your job are mundane and you feel there's nothing to look forward to, then identify something else to look forward to. If there is no satisfaction in your work, then focus on an activity or event after work that will make rising worthwhile. Sure, you have to go to work, but at the end of that workday is the event you've been waiting for. Getting up on time is the first step toward leaving work on time in order to get to your anticipated event.

Don't blame yourself for wanting to stay asleep. It helps to understand that the desire to stay asleep in the morning is a result of the built-in chemical conflict mentioned earlier. The chemicals that induce sleep are in conflict with those that are responsible for waking us up. If you were able each night to enjoy the amount of sleep you actually deserve, the sleep hormones would dissipate naturally. But as we force ourselves daily to conform to the working world's clocks, we must fight this constant battle.

A stress-free start to the day. One of the greatest benefits of allowing enough time to rise, prepare, and eat in a leisurely fashion is its impact over stress. By minimizing stress at the beginning of the day, you set a foundation of control, which helps combat stress during the rest of the day. Though stressful things may still happen, a relaxed start keeps the body and mind on a cool, level, and productive track.

Many people put off getting up until it's absolutely necessary, preferring to snatch just a few more minutes of half-sleep from the advancing morning. They will argue that it's not possible, that there's just not enough time to get up and out that quickly, especially if other family members are involved. When they finally get up, they immediately hit a critical path, which you'll remember from Chapter 3 is a bad thing, since every activity on a critical path is so closely tied to the next that even the slightest delay in one causes delay and stress. Breakfast is rushed, preparing is rushed, and they curse the traffic that's making them late.

So what if you were to redefine what was absolutely necessary, and build that back into your morning routine? Suppose you were to do an inventory of the activities that go into an average morning. List them, and get a sense of the time they take. And be realistic. Avoid optimistic estimates, such as "five minutes to make and eat breakfast" or "half an hour commuting if the roads are perfectly clear," and also allow time for seasonal surprises such as scraping ice off the car windshield or road construction. Do you have to prepare the kids for school, walk the dog, deal with busy transit centers?

This list will calculate the total amount of time required to get on your way in Cool Time, with little or no stress. It will give you a realistic rising time, a workable agenda.[2]

At this point, many people shake their heads. You can't predict all of these things so consistently," they say. "Some days the traffic may be great, but other days it's terrible. One day my kids will eat their food, and the next day they refuse. To which the answer is, "that's exactly the point. You can predict most of these things and expect the rest. So why not allow for them in your morning project plan?"

Adding a few minutes to each morning item generally adds no more than half an hour to the entire project. Imagine getting up just half an hour earlier to enjoy a stress-free start to the day. Ultimately, you can make your entire day much, much better by giving yourself the time you need to get it started on the right foot. And that, it seems, is worth much more than a few more minutes in bed.

TRAVEL TWICE, JOURNEY ONCE

This is an adaptation of the carpenter's maxim, "Measure twice, cut once." There is a great opportunity for effective time management in the way that you travel. Often people forget to factor travel time into their schedules, or if they do, they don't factor in enough. Trying to get across a city at one in the afternoon will be far more difficult than at one in the morning. These people are more prone to have accidents and experience road rage.

There will always be constraints to travel—construction, traffic jams, accidents, other drivers, the capabilities of your car, the weather.

---

2 A list to help calculate your optimum stress-free morning is available in the Cool-Time Action Plan at www.cool-time.com.

These things are out there, regardless of where you are going. Expect them. Plan for them. Allow them to happen. There will also always be impudent drivers whose behavior is outrageous, selfish, and illegal. They are also a constraint whose presence must be accepted. You cannot change the fact that they are there. It's better and healthier to allow for them and plan around them.

Going somewhere? Call first! There is nothing worse than traveling to an appointment only to find out your host has forgotten or, worse, is not there. Things happen. People get double-booked, and mistakes can be made, especially if the original agreement to meet was made during casual conversation. Memories of this sort, just like the memories that new business leads might have of you, have a half-life. The act of scheduling a meeting should, by default, include a confirmation call scheduled for one business week prior. This call should not only confirm the appointment, but could also include asking about nearest cross-streets, available parking, security procedures, exact location of the first meeting point, and emergency contact numbers.

Check your knowledge base. This is one of the areas where a knowledge base pays off handsomely. Just prior to your meeting you can load up your mind with news, concepts, and notes pulled from your constantly updated knowledge base.

Apply your Cool Time road plan to air travel. Being required to check in for your flight an hour or two before boarding may seem to be an intrusion into your busy day, but it's a fact of modern life and can often be a blessing in disguise. The airport departure lounge can be your private office away from the distractions of the workplace, a quiet spot to get great work done. With noise-reducing headphones, even the pressurized environment of the plane itself can be turned into a zone of quiet, reasonable comfort for either work or personal time en route.

Don't sacrifice eating. Include time for a meal in your travel plans for all the reasons discussed in Chapter 12.

HOW DO YOU SPELL RELIEF?

Do you ever marvel at the number of ads on TV that sell stomach remedies for heartburn and other discomforts? If more people allowed more time to eat more slowly, including extra time to choose better food, there would be much less need for these products. Our obsession with speed is literally burning us up.

Enjoy the ride. Hey, a trip to a client's office is time you can't get back. Whether it's one hour or six, stress-free travel time is healthier and more productive than a nerves-on-end frantic dash. Let your travel time become a small pleasure in the middle of your day rather than simply a means to an end.

In the end, practicing Cool Time is not an exercise in punctuality for punctuality's sake. It is a shrewd tool of business, one that allows you to remain in command of yourself first and foremost, and subsequently to gain control of your surroundings and the attention of the people in them. It's about striving for excellence. It's the ability to walk into a meeting or interview with confidence, putting your best self forward; about recalling key facts and ideas from your experience, your research and your knowledge base. It's about being able to focus on the right things to say; being able to strategize, calculate, think on your feet, prioritize, and impress with no need for apologies or self-deprecating jokes. It's about maintaining a clarity of purpose, and taking full advantage of all opportunities that arise from your efforts and preparation. It's about keeping your mind receptive to new ideas and new learning opportunities, and keeping your relationships balanced and positive. Your attitude and enthusiasm are a direct reflection of your leadership style. Cool Time is about leading a successful life.

CHAPTER 14
IMPLEMENTATION:
GETTING THERE FROM HERE

CHANGING THE STATUS QUO

SPACE TRAVEL FOR ANTS

The light-year is a term used to measure distances in space, and refers to how far something traveling at the speed of light could go in one calendar year. Since light travels at approximately 186,000 miles per second, a light-year works out to about 5,880,000,000,000 miles. Even light from the sun takes eight minutes or so to reach Earth.

Traveling across galaxies therefore poses a monstrous challenge, since the voyage would last much longer than any crew member's lifetime. But that's only true, say some scientists, if you look at space the way we look at everything else—in three dimensions.

Imagine yourself instead as an ant, standing on one end of a rubber mat. To get to the other end, there's only one thing to do:

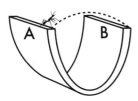

You walk along the surface of the mat until you get to the other end. But suppose that rubber mat were bent into a U-shape. As an ant, with no awareness of the third dimension, you would still be forced to walk the length of the mat, down into the base of the U and then back up the other side, unaware that a simple leap from point A to point B would be much faster and more efficient. That's what many quantum physicists feel is the secret to space travel: Rather than crossing the horizontal distance, we must learn to see our galactic neighborhood in a different dimension, in which the shortcuts may be right under our collective nose.

Back here on Earth, the rubber mat analogy is an invitation for you to consider the third I-word, the one that turns ideas into action. That word is implementation. Implementation means practice and change, both of which can be formidable obstacles. It challenges the attitude of "That's how we've always done it." If meetings are a major source of time wastage (as many people say they are), then change how they're run. If customers or colleagues expect you to work on three things at once, then change their understanding and expectations of you. If commuting is a daily horror, then change how it's done. Possibly one of the most difficult things about implementing new habits is getting them accepted by colleagues, clients, managers, and family. A fear of rocking the boat or appearing strange is a powerful disincentive toward putting efficient techniques into action.

Cool Time gives you the power to break free of the two-dimensional rubber-mat status quo to look for new avenues of positive achievement and proactive thinking.

- If you are the chairperson of the next meeting, then start applying Cool Time meeting principles. If you are not the chairperson, then find out who is and ask that person "Where's the agenda?" "Who is the timekeeper?" "Who are you inviting?"
- If you want to get more out of your day, then start using an I-Beam Agenda and keystone time, but make sure to let your people know what these things are and how they would benefit—what's in it for them.
- Construct your voicemail messages to guide callers, to manage their expectations, and satisfy their needs without sacrificing your precious working minutes, even if you've never done it before.

WHAT "CHANGE" AND "TRANSITION" MEAN

Most people are afraid of new things. They'd rather stick with what they have. "It may not be the best system," they say, "but we know how it works." That's human nature. It's nature, period. No sense in sticking your neck out into the unknown when it's perfectly safe here.

But at the same time, humans are inherently innovative. We experiment and we learn. Both forces are at work within your corporate village.

When new habits are introduced into the community, they often fail because "change," which refers to the new external event—the new procedure, the new thing—is brought in with no accompanying plan for "transition," which is the internal process of psychological reorientation that each human must now undergo.

When a new regime or behavior is introduced, let's say the fifty-five-minute meeting concept from Chapter 8, the people who introduce it focus more on getting the changes accomplished than on getting people used to them. "From now on," they say, "meetings will last only fifty-five minutes. There will be a timekeeper, and the chairperson will have to circulate the agenda a day in advance."

That's not going to work. It will fail.

You have to let people let go of the past gradually. They may be fearful and want to go back to the way things used to be. "We've always run meetings a certain way since before you came along." They may move forward with your idea, but with reluctance, waiting to see what happens to you—the "you first" scenario.

It may be necessary to transition our colleagues to buy in and observe the benefits slowly for themselves. This is why this book puts so much emphasis on influence, conditioning, and payback. Human comfort is the currency of change.

Adaptive capacity is the single most important attribute of successful leaders.

—Warren Bennis

THE BEST PRACTICES MEETING

A best practices meeting is a great way to introduce change into the workplace, since it allows for description, then discussion, negotiation, and finally an action plan. It's your opportunity to practice collective conditioning. Your colleagues can get used to the idea of a new habit, and their concerns can be acknowledged.

- *Give it appropriate meeting time.* Whether you call a meeting dedicated to the topic of changing a specific habit, or include it as an agenda item in an upcoming meeting, ensure that it is given the attention and time it deserves.
- *Describe the intended change.* What is it about current procedure you propose to change?
- *Describe the reasons for the change.* Why now? Why at all?
- *Describe the expected benefits of the change.* Tell the company, the client, and the individuals in the room what the benefits of the change will be.
- *Identify case studies or examples to support your proposition.* People don't like feeling they are moving into uncharted territory. They need to see proof that it has worked for others.
- *Describe your expected time line for change.* Recognize that change doesn't happen overnight. There may be a 100-day or more time line to consider.
- *Ask for input, positive and negative, from the group.* Addressing their concerns and objections gets them out on the table and is the first step toward acceptance and forward movement. This, by the way, is most effective when the meeting agenda has been sent out in advance of the meeting (as per the fifty-five-minute meeting guidelines in Chapter 8). Attendees will have time to properly channel emotions rather than deal with them for the first time during the meeting.
- *Propose a pilot project.* Sometimes it is best to define the change activity as a pilot project, which gives participants the security of knowing if it doesn't work out, they can return to what they know. This type of "escape route" is common to many of the Cool Time initiatives, since it meets people's basic comfort concerns.

- *Form an action plan with a time line.* Create a plan that outlines how the new habit will be rolled out. For example, if the department were to adopt keystone times for all of the team, how would that affect other meetings, phone calls, etc.? Adopting a policy in which keystone time can be reserved between 9:00 A.M. and noon only, and meetings booked between 1:00 P.M. and 4:00 P.M. only might be a generally workable approach.
- *Establish benchmarks and review times.* It's not enough just to set sail. Your team will need to regroup on a regular basis to review the success or challenges that this rollout has presented. All best practices, whether team-wide or just between you and your manager, need scheduled review and benchmarking. Similarly, without regular review, it is easy for people to revert to old habits before the new ones stick.

THE ROLE MODEL

Nothing succeeds like success in these matters. Look for a role model in your office—someone who has already adopted the same type of best practices, whether consciously or after years of experience. Have her present at the best practices meeting, or at least summarize why she does what she does.

At all times, when educating adults in new habits, it is always necessary to allow them to come to their own conclusions if buy-in is to happen at all.

EMOTIONAL BEDROCK: BUILDING ON STONE

Cool Time principles within this book are neither difficult nor revolutionary. They consist of straightforward techniques in planning, communication, and working within the constraints of life. They also require an investment in time as well as conviction. People's expectations and emotions must be managed proactively if they are to buy into your plan. But, as with all good investments, the end result will have a greater payoff than the initial outlay; otherwise it would not be worth doing.

In the real world, stone has been used as a solid building material for thousands of years. From the foundation up to the turrets, it has always been one of our strongest resources. Yet stone can also be carved and manipulated to fit the needs of the builder. It can support, yet conform to new shapes.

Bedrock, for example, is a solid layer of dense rock just below the Earth's surface, upon which large buildings can be reliably constructed. Without it, a structure can slowly sink.

For the purposes of establishing Cool Time, "emotional bedrock" refers to an inner conviction that what we are doing is right; that the techniques, such as project management, upon which this book is built are time-honored and proven. This solid conviction gives us the confidence to move forward, the stability to embrace change.

When it's time to explain to your manager why you want to establish keystone time, or why your estimation of a project's time line is longer than she'd hoped, or why you insist that a meeting start and end at its posted time, this is when you can stand on this rock-solid conviction, this emotional bedrock, this understanding that the principles are right and that they do work. You can remind your manager that you're both on the same side. Your mutual desire is improved productivity without added cost. You can also remind her (and yourself) that you are not alone. There are hundreds of thousands of professionals out there for whom a calculated, intelligent, and cool approach to time management has already enhanced their collective lives in so many areas, such as productivity, reduced absenteeism and turnover, quality of communications, management, morale, customer retention, and, of course, a healthier balance sheet.

BUILDING A STAIRWAY

It is easier to climb a staircase than scale a wall. Similarly, success in implementing change will come through incremental advancement rather than a single wholesale adjustment.

Any of the Cool Time techniques you choose to undertake will be best achieved in small steps. At the gym, for example, your instructor will point out that the secret to a successful workout schedule, especially one that is brand new to your lifestyle, is one in which you start small— using lighter weights, shorter running distances, and briefer workout periods—gradually increasing and building on prior victories to allow your body and your schedule time to adjust and truly benefit.

If you were to go back to your office tomorrow and start to make major changes to the routine, there would probably be great resistance, not because the ideas are perceived as bad, necessarily, just that they're different from what currently exists. Such rejection would be difficult for you, too, deflating your newfound optimism, putting yet another good idea out of reach, leaving another how-to book upon the shelf.

So start small. Make your improvements slowly over time, constantly communicating and sharing the "win-win," appealing to the comfort concerns of your colleagues, and selling the benefits at every turn.

The same applies to you. Even if a Cool Time concept makes great sense and you can hardly wait to get started, it may be better if you take your time. If your calendar is booked solid for the next month, then small changes may be possible, but there may be no opportunity to make major changes such as regularly scheduled opportunity time, or establishing regular I-Beam Reviews and I-Beam Bases. But you can at least mark them into your calendar for the upcoming month and, in the interim, attempt smaller victories to start getting into the habit of defending your time against the current internal and external pressures of your life.

TEST AND MEASURE

In building a stone structure, a craftsman uses certain tools, including a plumb line, to constantly check and recheck that the stones are perpendicular and conforming to plan. This is not done just once, but constantly throughout the building process.

So it is with the establishment of new habits: At all times, remember to test and measure. How do you recognize progress unless you have something to compare it to? And how can you compare it if you do not give yourself time to do so? This is why the I-Beam Base exists—to allow time for continual improvement. And why the benchmarking meetings need to be scheduled after the best practices meeting—to actively seek additional benefit for yourself by reviewing which of the Cool Time principles work for you, which don't, and which need adjustment. This is why even the most successful athletes spend time in practice—to ensure that improvement is always a top priority, as they measure how far they have actually come.

CHAPTER 14

DEVELOPING HABITS: THE TWENTY-ONE-DAY RULE

THE CATAPULT

If you've ever operated a pocket catapult or a slingshot, the type with a Y-shaped handle and an elastic band for launching, you already know one simple fact of operation: To propel an object forward, you have to start by pulling backward. To make the tool work effectively, you have to move back one step, that is, by pulling and tensioning the band before you can propel the object forward.

To make use of a practical plan, to win back your time, to influence others, we need to take a couple of steps back first by planning, explaining, selling, or influencing. One step back for many steps forward. Without it, your plan—your projectile—will fall limply at your feet.

It takes twenty-one days for an action to move from a conscious undertaking to force of habit. This is another reason why people often fall off the wagon when it comes to making changes in their lives: They don't stick with it long enough. Twenty-one days is a full working month—four five-day weeks. This is why pilot projects and benchmarking make such great sense. You might want to choose a quieter month of the year, if there is such a thing, to roll out your changes. Remember the principle of the reserved activity in Chapter 3. Enter your keystone times and your I-Beam Agenda activities now into your calendar for each business day into the future. Even if you have to edit or reschedule them, they'll be there, waiting for you, ready for the work that is to come.

THE POWER OF RITUAL

Once new practices have been introduced and "sold" to your community, you can allow the procedures to settle themselves, like mortar, holding stones in place. You can take full advantage of the human preference for rhythm and ritual to establish a comfortable sequence of activities, such as an I-Beam Review scheduled for the same time each day, or an hour of keystone time assigned to every afternoon of the week.

Ritual not only makes action consistent, it has also been shown to manipulate moods. This goes back to our very first weeks of life when rituals of feeding, playing, and bedtime were first introduced, laying a strong foundation for the people that we were to become. Ritual and repetition make us feel secure. Energy and enthusiasm are more readily accessed when activities are planned, anticipated, and made to fit into a routine. This, in turn, delivers the mental energy required for top-level performance. It taps once again into the age-old core of our being.

On a personal level, start by establishing great sleep rituals, then add exercise and eating rituals; going to bed the same time every night; getting up the same time every morning; exercising at the same time each day; eating meals at the same time each day. These are the types of beneficial activities that your body will pick up on and will gravitate toward. You will find that benefits come quickly to the forefront— benefits such as greater stamina, greater energy, better digestion, better sleep, a greater sensation of well-being. These all make you feel great, and also vastly improve your productivity, expertise, and attractiveness.

Use the patterning and planning techniques in Chapter 3 to map out your weeks as far in advance as possible, to allow time for these rhythmic elements to become part of, and then influence, your calendar and everyone who is involved with it.

WRITE YOUR PLAN

Just as the architect arrives before the stonecutter, so should your plan be committed to paper (or on screen). As we have discussed, hazy notions are no match for real, hard copy plans since they offer no chance for revision and reality.

Have you ever noticed just how many problems can be solved just by telling someone about them? Professionals such as psychiatrists, psychologists, counselors, and coaches certainly have their own expertise to deliver, but a great deal of the catharsis and healing can simply come from hearing yourself describe it to another human being. This is what a plan can do. It's your opportunity to "speak" your thoughts and hear yourself say them. Many of the problems or obstacles will then be revealed for your own diagnosis and resolution.

Commit your plan and your goals to paper or on screen on your computer. Allow yourself the opportunity to make your new habits real in your mind by seeing them scheduled. Whether it's planning an I-Beam Base at the end of each workday or writing down your five-year goals, this is your blueprint for satisfaction and success.

THE CREDIT CARD

If you have a credit card with a large balance and you make just the minimum payment every month—let's say $100—what are you actually doing? You are taking $100 out of your paycheck to service a debt that continues to grow. For as long as that $100 is being used to pay interest on an existing debt, no progress is being made. Now let that $100 represent your creative energy—energy that could have otherwise been used to make the difference between a good job interview and a winning job interview; a good proposal and a great proposal, a good mark on an exam or a top mark on an exam. As long as your creative energy is being used to keep track of existing tasks and priorities, it is just servicing a time debt; it is not free to be used to its maximum potential, to move your thoughts, plans, and activities from adequate to outstanding.

To break free, you have to commit to a change, to eliminate debts of all sorts as fast as possible. At the early stages, your goal will seem very far away. It seems too different, too radical, the benefits too distant. And that's what holds so many people back from achieving so much. The benefits *will* come, and they *will* start to reveal themselves, slowly at first but with greater and greater solidity as your debts decrease and your power increases. Success *can* happen, but one step at a time.

THE OPEN-DOOR POLICY

One of the most pervasive and well-intentioned traditions in the workplace is the open-door policy (ODP). Whether you have an office with a real door or a cubicle with three walls, the mantra is that you should be available and accessible to your colleagues at all times. Well, too much of a good thing quickly turns into a bad thing. An open-door policy that exists for the full day turns people into doormats for whom no control over time and work exists. Uncontrolled interruptions mean they must make up for lost time after hours.

There has to be a happy medium, one in which your door is open for most of the day, say 80 percent, but closed for the other 20 percent during your keystone time so that real work can get done.

Keystone time is described in Chapter 6, so there's no need to repeat it here. But how do you introduce a revised open-door policy? By communicating it to those it will most affect—your subordinates and your boss—and by introducing change over time.

Such gradual development will allow the status quo to change slowly and confidently, which means the only impediment left to successful time management will be you.

CHAPTER 15
YOUR ACHILLES' HEEL: PERSONAL OBSTACLES TO IMPLEMENTATION

THE MAN WHO ALMOST SOLD THE EIFFEL TOWER

In 1925 a confidence man by the name of Victor Lustig invited a group of wealthy scrap-metal merchants to a chic hotel in Paris to discuss the sale and dismantling of the Eiffel Tower. Posing as a representative of the French government, he described how the tower had become a financial failure, and explained that he had been authorized to solicit bids from select companies for its purchase and removal. After a few weeks Mr. Lustig contacted the winning bidder, and invited him to another hotel to hand over the cash in exchange for the deed of ownership. But something about Mr. Lustig's manner triggered suspicion in the prospective buyer's mind. Why were they always meeting in hotels? Why did he work alone? Could this be a scam?

Sensing the suspicion, Mr. Lustig changed tactics. Rather than focusing on the grandiose plans of his government, he made small talk about how he was but an underpaid civil servant, and how perhaps the deal could be made a little sweeter for the buyer if just a little of the money went under the table.

The buyer was now convinced that Mr. Lustig was indeed a representative of the government. After all, in his experience, all the people he had dealt with in government had been corrupt to one degree or another, so indeed Mr. Lustig must be the genuine article. The money changed hands.

When the truth about Mr. Lustig's identity eventually came out, and that the tower had never been for sale, the buyer was too embarrassed to step forward. Lustig and the cash disappeared.[1]

Your desire to regain control of time will have to pass a number of tests, some of which are part of your own makeup. Victor Lustig knew that human attributes and frailties are always present, and must always be accounted for. He made a career out of that knowledge. Your knowledge of your "self," your human self, is equally important, if your time management plans are to succeed; and therefore this chapter looks at some of the most common personality issues that present real, but not insurmountable, obstacles to successful implementation.

THE SUPERHERO SYNDROME

The superhero syndrome results when the pressures of numerous tasks and projects lead to a perception that everything must be done by you and you alone. You feel you are the only one who can do it properly. There's nowhere else to turn. You've got to do it all.

As a superhero, you have some great gifts: You have energy and drive. You have far-ranging plans and expectations as well as high standards. You enjoy responsibility and accountability, and enjoy taking things on. And the common ideology is expressed in the phrase, "If you want something done right, you've got to do it yourself."

The Cool Time approach is to invite the superhero to consider which is more important: Doing the task, or getting the task done? The solution may be not in doing all the parts yourself, but in making sure the right people are chosen to do parts for you. As Jim Collins states in his landmark book *Good to Great*, "it's a matter of getting the right people on the bus."[2] And that's where delegation comes in.

---

1 Robert Greene, *The 48 Laws of Power* (New York: Viking, 1998).
2 James C. Collins, *Good to Great: Why Some Companies Make the Leap ... and Others Don't* (New York: HarperBusiness, 2001).

INEFFECTIVE DELEGATION

Delegation doesn't come easily to people, especially superheroes. Not only is it difficult to let go of tasks that they can easily do, they always worry that the tasks will not be done to the same level of perfection that the superheroes expect of themselves. This becomes a self-fulfilling prophecy when a task is assigned to an unprepared candidate. The candidate makes a mess of it, and the superhero perceives that as proof that delegation doesn't work

Delegation, though, is an exercise in effective leadership and education, and is built on investment in the capabilities and potential of an entire department. Productivity is compounded when you allow numerous people to work in parallel toward a goal.

First, delegation frees you up to do the things that mean the most. It's the 80/20 rule again. Just because you can do all the tasks involved in a project doesn't mean you *should* be doing them all. It's essential that you focus on the top 20 percent of tasks that yield the greatest reward.

Second, delegation develops skills and loyalty in staff. Most people love to learn. A stimulating environment that provides opportunities for people to expand and further their skills can be a powerful motivator, and in some cases worth more than financial compensation when it comes to loving a job and deciding to stay. By entrusting your staff with new responsibilities, you help to ensure a vibrant and loyal support team, which sets the stage for further productivity.

Third, delegation is a hallmark of leadership. When you delegate, you are demonstrating trust, which, as Edwin Bliss says, is quite different from saying, "Do what I tell you."[3]

It's essential, however, to choose and support the right person, and it's equally essential that the person be given time to learn. Many people make the mistake of interpreting delegation as simply dumping a task upon someone. If this person *is* underqualified, then he *will* fail.

Though your immediate priority may be the quick completion of a current task, remember that proactive delegation is an exercise in

---

3 Edwin Bliss, *Getting Things Done: Timesaving Strategies That Make the Most of Your Day* (New York: Scribner 1976).

education to set the stage for future time savings, thanks to a well-trained, confident, and reliable support team.

It's a three-step process. (Remember the catapult analogy in Chapter 14—you've got to move backwards a little in order to move forwards a lot.)

- *Step 1: Do 100 percent of the job yourself, and make sure the "apprentice" is observing and learning.* This means you end up doing the work, which you would have resigned yourself to doing anyway as someone who dislikes or distrusts delegation.

  When instructing your support person, assume nothing. Ask him to repeat your instructions. This is not being patronizing; it forms part of effective communication and the establishment of mutual commitment.

- *Step 2: On the next round, expect to do 50 percent of the job yourself while the apprentice tries it out.* Observe and provide feedback. If he performed the task correctly, then, in addition to a little praise, explore with him why he did it as he did. This sheds light on how the task was approached and helps to determine if he can perform this task consistently.

  If he did not do the task correctly, it becomes an opportunity to explore what went wrong, primarily by asking questions and listening. Telling people what to do or what they did wrong develops a false assumption that the person understands. The only way you know why they were not successful is to get them to explain why they did what they did.

- *Step 3: By the third round, the apprentice should be able to do 95 percent of the job, with you only coming in to finish it off to your standards.* Again, review, praise, and clarification are essential.

Obviously this exercise is not a quick one, but it's the wisest way to facilitate successful delegation.

Upon handing over the task to him, you will be free to focus your energies upon more appropriate tasks with a genuine sense of confidence.

Make sure, however, that your trained delegatee has both the necessary authority to work on your behalf, as well as access to an appropriate "answer-person" to avoid delay and hesitation brought on by indecisiveness or fear of making a mistake.

When delegating, beware of over-reliance on a star player. Often in an organization where numerous projects happen concurrently, one person emerges who is very capable of performing certain tasks or undertaking certain responsibilities. This person becomes, in the minds of all project managers, the star player without whom no project will be successful. The dangers of depending on a star player become immediately apparent the day she suddenly becomes unavailable. Preferential treatment given to these stars is also damaging to the solidarity of a team, all of which points to an additional benefit of developing and nurturing your support team through proactive delegation.

Delegation is not about palming off tasks mechanically to a subordinate who has no choice in the matter. It is more about making wise choices in terms of the allocation of your own time, the effective completion of projects and tasks, and the development of the abilities and attitudes of your support team. This combines the concepts of continual improvement, leadership, and training. A little time invested in stepping back and teaching has far greater value than the same time spent simply charging ahead as a slave to the urgency of an overstuffed schedule.

OVERCONFIDENCE

Whereas the superhero syndrome deals with the belief that you alone *must* do it all, overconfidence is the internal conviction that you *can* do it all, and that there's nothing you can't do. It's not so much a pressure thing as merely confidence in your own abilities that exceeds the realities of your schedule. This may be great for the ego, but can lead to great stress.

Just like superheroes, overconfident people do best when their confidence and abilities are focused on the right tasks at the right times, identified through planning, prioritization, and delegation. A Roman administrator named Publius Syrius said it first in 42 BC, and it still rings true today: "Never promise more than you can perform."

CHAPTER 15

UNREALISTIC TIME ESTIMATES

A major source of personal schedule overload comes from underestimating how long a task will take. In thinking through the expected duration of a task, it is human nature to err on the side of optimism by allotting the amount of time that you *hope* it will take, rather than the amount of time it will probably take.

Such well-intentioned but ill-fated expectations can quickly push a person's day onto the critical path. In an effort to please clients, managers, or teammates, promised delivery times are earlier than is truly possible. Sometimes these deadlines are met through much sweat, stress, and toil. Other times, the bad news has to be delivered that things are going to be late. It's better to give the stakeholder a realistic expectation up front, one that you might be able to exceed, than it is to give them false hopes followed by disappointment.

The simplest approach to this is to take an educated estimate of a task's duration and double it. Things seldom, if ever, take the amount of time you hope they would. By factoring in this extra time in the first place, you stand a better chance of completing the task within realistic time lines. If all goes well, and you finish early, you'll have time left over for other tasks and you'll look like a hero. If things take a little longer, however, it's healthy and smart to have that extra time.

PUTTING THINGS IN CONCRETE TERMS

Modern-day project management owes a lot of its practical success from large-scale construction projects in the U.S. during the 1950s and 1960s, such as the U.S. Navy's Polaris Missile Program and DuPont's cement factory construction. These helped develop a philosophy of estimation known as PERT (Program Evaluation and Review Technique). It included a calculation for estimating job duration that went like this: P = Pessimistic: How long the project would take if almost everything had problems; O = Optimistic: How long the project would take if everything went perfectly; R = Realistic:

How long the project will probably take, based on the estimates of experienced project managers.

These were then added together and averaged using a formula to calculate a result weighted more toward the pessimistic. This gave project planners the confidence and realistic backing to plan the project and explain it to the stakeholders.

THE LAST-MINUTE CLUB

There is a certain group of people for whom all of this planning stuff just doesn't wash. They swear that their best work is done when they're facing the deadline square on, when the chips are down, when the pressure is highest. If your creativity and brilliance comes from the high pressure of fast-looming deadlines, then that's a strength, not a weakness.

But let's make sure first. Let's make sure the reasons for your pride in being a "last-minute type" aren't tied up in the murky world of procrastination. Then we'll be free to look at options for making your strength a super-strength.

PROCRASTINATION

When it comes down to getting tasks done, there will always be at least one that you just don't want to do. It may hold the least appeal to you, it may be the least rewarding, or it may involve confrontation, unpleasant tasks, or drudgery. It also makes every other task on your list look instantly more appealing.

Unfortunately, in addition to weighing heavily on your schedule, procrastination fills your heart and mind with negative energy. The longer you procrastinate, the longer you live with a shadow of guilt, dread, and the pang of the inevitable. There is a constant awareness of the task that remains unstarted.

The only way to deal with procrastination is to get the task done *as soon as is both possible and proper*. The I-Beam Agenda and prioritization techniques discussed earlier provide the tools to step back and assess this task in relation to the others. Is it important enough and urgent enough to be done right away, even though you really don't want to do it, or can it be legitimately scheduled for a later time? What about delegation? Could or should this task be assigned to somebody else who has the time, skills, or experience to take it off your hands?

Why are you procrastinating in the first place? The reasons vary with people and circumstances, but identifying the cause is the first step in breaking the pattern:

- *Size*: Is the task too large to complete in one go? Are you waiting for a large block of time to get it done completely? Then try breaking it up. Use your project planning skills to break an overly large task into sub-parts. Use carryover momentum (see Chapter 6) to work on it regularly and incrementally.
- *Vagueness*: The project is too big or vague to contemplate. Create a project plan on paper. Get a sense of timing and priority by lining up the component tasks backwards from the due date to the latest possible start date (the critical path), and then factor in lead times. By putting the plan down on paper, the start and end points turn into tangible, visible elements, which allows you to envision what is needed to get it completed.
- *Lack of guidance*: Is there no procedure or set of guidelines in place to show how to go about the task? Are you unsure of the right thing to do? Then seek help. Find a mentor, a tutor, someone who can deliver not only the how-to's but also the wisdom of experience.
- *Fear and anxiety*: Are you avoiding a task because you are afraid of it or of the results? Many people avoid medical and dental checkups for this reason. This is a classic case of fear of the unknown. Confront the fear. It is better to know than not know because knowing opens the door to solutions. If fear is causing procrastination, then identify what it is you're worried about. Write it down—get it out of your head. Then write down all the possible consequences of the fear, and next to each what the cure or resolution would be. You'll be amazed how helpful it is to see the entire situation laid out before you. You'll regain control.

- *Perfectionism*: Do you feel that if the task can't be done completely and perfectly, then it's not worth starting? Refer back to the Size paragraph above. Work on doing smaller parts of the project as perfectly as possible.
- *Boredom*: Is the task just too plain boring or unpleasant, making anything else look more appealing? Then use the productive procrastination technique. When you have a task that you don't want to do, other tasks always look far more appealing, so do those other tasks first. You might want to consider such an outlook as a way of getting everything else done. Provided that the task being procrastinated is not *vitally* urgent, you might want to take advantage of productive procrastination to get some of your other chores completed. This makes positive use of your time and turns a weakness (procrastination) into a strength (achievement). Also, you will have cleared your schedule to allow space for the original procrastinated task.

There is a difference between rescheduling something and procrastination. Procrastination is an emotional act in which you avoid doing something that needs to be done because is causes discomfort. Rescheduling is a logical act in which you move tasks based on urgency and prioritization issues. Whatever it is that's making you put off completing a task, it is usually better and healthier to get it done if you *know* it needs to be done now. Consider these approaches:

- *Do it first. Get it over with.* If it's important enough to get done now, then do it now and let your mind and body enjoy the freedom from an unpleasant task rather than the dread of procrastination. Once the time is right to take on the task, do it. If it keeps getting put off for weeks or months, it's time to question its relevance and/or to find someone else to do it.
- *Focus on the finish.* Envision the task as already completed. Picture, in your mind, the end result of the chore and the feeling it gives you to see it finished. Buy into its existence so that its completed state becomes real in your imagination. By picturing your unpleasant task in its completed state, you focus your mind, your energies, and your determination.

- *Focus on the step after the finish.* There's always more sky on the other side of the mountain. If a task is particularly unpleasant, such as having to deliver bad news, then focus your involvement in the healing process that follows. Even though you may be the bearer of bad news, that shouldn't stop you from presenting the first steps of the "next chapter," becoming the catalyst for healing. If the task is merely undesirable, such as a dental appointment from 10:00A.M. to 11:00A.M., recognize that there is life after 11:00A.M.. You'll be back doing other things. The pain will pass. The undesired activity is finite.
- *Give yourself a deadline.* Focus is a powerful thing. Give your mind a fixed duration, a finish line rather than a hazy goal, and mark off every step, every small victory along the way.
- *Give yourself a reward.* Perhaps this means going home early, or buying yourself something, or moving on to a different task, one that you'd rather do. A reward is a powerful incentive to counter the forces of procrastination. Like icing on the cake, the reward seems doubly pleasurable since your conscience will be clear, and the weight of the onerous task will have been lifted from your shoulders.
- *Delegate it to someone.* Maybe the task would best be done by someone else, maybe someone who actually enjoys it.
- *Do the easiest part first.* If the task has many parts, and you're not sure where to start, then start with the easiest part. The feeling of accomplishment and momentum generated by this activity will then attune your mind and body to the rest of the task. This is particularly useful if you're trying to write a report and you're suffering from writer's block. Just write whatever comes to mind in a stream-of-consciousness style. Once those first few ideas are released from short-term memory, the next batch will flow in.
- *Consider the cost of putting it off.* As unattractive as a task may be, what would be the consequences of procrastination? Lost business? Fines or penalties? Ruined relationships? The cost of procrastination can have long-term repercussions.
- *Accept the inevitable.* Some things just have to get done. The sooner you take the bull by the horns, the sooner you can get past the unpleasant task and on to the things you prefer. Time spent procrastinating is not pleasurable time. It is hard time. Life is too short to allow hours or days

to be spent under the cloud of looming guilt. The value, the pleasure, the release that is felt upon completion of an unpleasant task moves you back onto a healthy track of achievement and self-determination.

THE LAST-MINUTE CLUB (CONTINUED)

OK, so you still say your preference for working to the last minute is not rooted in procrastination. You just do better work that way. Great! Use that strength to your advantage, but consider factoring these pointers in your plan:

- *Move your deadline up to accommodate the unexpected.* It's great to capitalize on adrenaline-fueled creativity by working to a late deadline, but what if your printer jams or the e-mail gets returned or the courier misplaces your package? Any number of snafus can threaten an otherwise excellent piece of work, and can bring on additional stress, delay, and damage. Why let simple procedure threaten to ruin your masterpiece? Experienced last-minuters strongly suggest moving the deadline date up by a day (or some appropriate amount) as soon as you take on the project. Work to this self-imposed deadline and take advantage of your need for urgency without losing out due to unforeseen minor glitches.
- *Consider the others on your team.* Though you might thrive on a midnight deadline, how does it affect others who are collaborating on the project? Are they as comfortable with this pressure? Does their role start only after your piece has been completed? This is not to suggest you sideline your preferences for theirs, but perhaps a little up-front planning and communication will allow all sides to use their skills to the advantage of the project. You may be working with these people on other projects after this one, and their understanding of and attitude toward your preferred working style will be formed pretty early on. Careful nurturing of these relationships will be the ticket to future successes.

Is working to the last minute a conscience-soother? A fatalistic self-justification that says, "Hey, I did the best I could. There was no more time"? We can look back at our school years as the breeding ground for this technique when we would procrastinate in working on papers and assignments for days or weeks, only to galvanize ourselves at the last minute into harried activity, all-nighters, and requests for extensions.

The solution is in a little back-planning and project management in which wishful thinking is replaced by clear vision. If a project must get done, then it must get done properly. The principles of *Kaizen*, keystone time, and project planning will be your greatest allies. Remember, the pressure to perform under last-minute conditions creates stress, which affects the very areas of the mind required for creative, intelligent thought. You have the power to decide whether you work with the positive stress of self-imposed short deadlines, or the negative stress of running out of time. Long after you've decided, the results of your work will remain for others to judge.

THE COAST GUARD RULE

The U.S. Coast Guard has a rule for fueling boats that epitomizes the type of thinking necessary for avoiding last-minute crunches: The top third of a tank is fuel for going out. The bottom third of the tank is fuel for coming back. The middle third is for surprises along the way.

WORKAHOLISM

There comes a point in which the value of the work undertaken becomes less than the amount of time put in. We've observed this in the principle of negative-value time (Chapter 12). When this becomes chronic, it's called workaholism, which is a bad thing.

There's a definite distinction between working hard, working overtime, and workaholism. Working hard is the diligent application of our energies and talents into tasks that have been properly identified, prioritized, and scheduled with minimal distraction or disruption. This is the kind of work that Cool Time is about, since it allows for maximized productivity without upsetting a healthy work–life balance.

Working overtime means putting in a few more hours than we should *once in a while*. There are occasions when working overtime has its rewards—meeting a deadline on a "crunch" project, or making some extra cash for the holidays, for example. The key is that overtime remains the exception rather than the norm.

Workaholism, though, isn't about hard work, it's about work addiction—compulsive overwork, whereas hard workers do what is needed to get a job done. Once it's done, they relax and allow time for family, friends, and reflection. They work long hours on a short-term basis with clear goals. But workaholics are preoccupied with work and are unable to turn it off. Most workaholics are not aware that they've crossed the boundary into inefficiency. Instead, they simply see themselves as relentless producers, focused on a distant goal that needs just a few more hours of work to complete.

The conditions that make workaholism possible are quite easy to see. North America's culture is based on a work ethic: You are what you do. Portable computers, cellular phones, and Internet access make working from anywhere, around the clock, easier than ever, and taps directly into that sense of urgency we discussed back in Chapter 2. There is also a fear factor—fear of not appearing to be a team player; fear of being left out of the loop; fear of taking a vacation in case you are replaced; fear of being part of the next round of downsizing. A combination of personal, technological, and social pressures conspires to create fertile ground for workaholism to flourish.

What are the signs of a workaholic? For a start, workaholics tend to work long hours, consistently staying late and coming in on weekends and holidays (or working from home on weekends and holidays), even if they do not have any pressing deadlines. They think about work constantly, even when they are not at work. As Dr. Bryan Robinson states, the workaholic "uses work to fulfill an inner need."[4] Workaholics rarely have hobbies, except those that are work-related, such as golf with colleagues. And they tend to neglect personal relationships, especially with spouses and children.

---

4 Bryan E. Robinson, Ph.D., *Chained to the Desk: A Guidebook for Workaholics, Their Partners and Children, and the Clinicians Who Treat Them* (New York: New York University Press, 1998).

Nor are workaholics great team players, since they have trouble delegating. They may enjoy taking care of a task themselves, living out a chronic case of the superhero syndrome, discussed earlier.

In general, workaholics' actions and priorities are inconsistent with true productivity. Workaholism is an addiction to work for work's sake. There is a tendency to gravitate toward time-consuming tasks and to work the longest hours on the least productive or least practical tasks, since workaholism is an addiction to work, not results. Workaholics tend to focus on tasks that are immediately visible, rather than establishing priority and then focusing on the top-ranked task.

The costs of workaholism: Having a workaholic on staff should be a source of immediate concern. Though she may appear as a paragon of busy-ness, a role model for the rest of the team, in actual fact the opposite is true. A workaholic environment creates stress, burnout, and low morale among all staff, since workaholics demand excessive work from subordinates, which results in sick leave and stress-related workers' compensation claims.

Similarly, the adrenaline that fuels much of a workaholic's activity was never meant to be used that way. Adrenaline is intended for fast escape—the fight-or-flight reflex. It's acidic. Over time, it destroys body cells and blood vessels.

If you think you might be a workaholic, the best thing to do is to aim for the win–win. The pleasure you derive from working hard is an asset. But it's essential to make sure that the efforts you undertake are correctly directed, and that balance is maintained.

Ask yourself:

- Is the work I'm doing truly top priority, or do I just need to feel busy?
- Can this work be done by someone else—that is, can it be delegated?
- Who will see the payoff of this work? Does it contribute to a key project?
- What am I sacrificing? Family? Health? Exercise?
- How are my habits affecting my staff? Are they getting frustrated trying to keep up? Is there high turnover?
- How uptight would I get if I went home with all of this stuff still left to do?

Workaholism is a personality-based addiction, encouraged through the pressures and demands of business. It is not a substance addiction, but the withdrawal symptoms might be similar: intense discomfort, frustration, and stress. If you identify yourself as a workaholic, you will need to admit that fact first, and then seek a pattern of change that you can handle. This primarily consists of a tangible project plan and a written collection of "balance" items such as family, friends and hobbies, and a time line for change.

It is also a condition that is not always taken seriously in the context of the North American work ethic, at least not until the paramedics have to be called.

The bottom line: Workaholism is not productivity, it's addiction to the sensation of work.

PRESENTEEISM

A similar concept that reflects many of the problems of a high-pressure, no-time workplace can be seen in the condition called "presenteeism." Identified by Manchester University professor Cary Cooper, it refers to a marked reduction in productivity due to stress, injury, or information overload, but in contrast to absenteeism where an employee stays home, presenteeism sees the employee coming to work while sick because of a heightened fear of losing his job, or simply as a "perverse expression of commitment."[5]

Obviously such a condition highlights the schism between what the body needs and what the work schedule demands. It is an impediment to clear thought, productivity, and communication, yet people still come to work and occupy space. Such situations send strong signals (or at least they should) that time and rest are the essential ingredients of productivity.

In a small sense, presenteeism might result in a delayed project because a staff member may not really be on the ball. In a larger sense, it may result in the running aground of an oil tanker, as happened with the *Exxon Valdez*

---

5 Graham Lowe, "Here in body, absent in productivity," *Canadian HR Reporter* (December 2, 2002), page 42.

in 1989, or a crew member forgetting to close the bow doors of a high-speed ferry as happened with the *Herald of Free Enterprise* in 1987.

Your body is a strict creditor. It takes back what it needs, regardless.

CHAPTER 16
ROADBLOCKS: ENVIRONMENTAL OBSTACLES TO IMPLEMENTATION

THE BUCKET BRIGADE

Imagine yourself standing in a yard along with some of your colleagues. There is a barrel of water in the corner of the yard and your task is to take the water from the barrel, transport it across the yard, and pour it into another barrel on the other side. There are no pumps or hoses available, and the full barrel is too heavy to lift, roll, or otherwise move. All you have is a single bucket.

It would seem that the most practical way to move the water would be for you and your colleagues to stand an arm's length apart, forming a human chain from the barrel up to the container. In this way, by passing the bucket from person to person, the water will be transported and you will all be paid.

Now, this will be a time-consuming process, but it's the only way to get the job done, and it *will* eventually get the job done. Besides, as each person is doing just a small part of the work, you will all share in a balance between work and rest. Furthermore, if the person at the end of the line pours the water into the container, then throws the empty bucket back down to the person at the barrel, half of the bucket-passing time can be saved.

This story serves as an analogy for identifying and dealing with the constraints of a given situation. Sure, you would be able to do better if there were more buckets on hand, or a hose, or a forklift truck to move the barrel, but all you have is a single bucket. Do you perceive that bucket as a tool that will help you get the water to its goal, or do you view the entire scenario as an impossible one? What about the colleagues at your disposal? How well will they work and cooperate? What about the weather and the available daylight? These are the constraints of your project.

Constraints are not a negative thing. Project constraints support success by illuminating a practical path. People who talk of personal fulfillment and goal setting generally speak of the kinds of things you can achieve if you apply your mind, your body, and your soul toward them. That's great, but blind enthusiasm alone will not suffice. You have to work with what you've got, play the cards you're dealt, and work within your boundaries. Constraints help to define those operating boundaries. They are credible markers of achievement and potential that come in very handy when the realities of life threaten to rob you of your optimism.

TIME: THE ULTIMATE CONSTRAINT

Time is fixed. There are twenty-four hours per day; no more, no less. There will always be another day. Not everything can be completed in a single day; in fact, it's a wasted effort to try. Planning and communication allow you to decide what should be completed today and what can be planned for tomorrow. There's only one of you, there's only one of me, and we each can do only one thing at a time.

YOU ARE YOUR OWN CONSTRAINT—AND THAT'S OK

You are a fixed commodity with a finite measure of energy. People who drive themselves beyond the limits of the body and brain find the repayment terms to be pretty strict (see "Presenteeism" in Chapter 15). If you work fourteen hours one day, don't expect to be able to give 100 percent the next day or the day after that. You just can't do it. Working beyond your allotted capacity invites reduced quality and performance, as well as burnout, illness, and injury. You are both your greatest asset and your greatest constraint.

YOUR PEOPLE ARE CONSTRAINTS

Your people, all the people you work with, are project constraints. And remember, the term "constraints" in a project management framework is not a negative thing. You can work only with what you have, and whatever you have defines your constraints. Whether you work in a large company or a small firm, or even if you are self-employed, you have to interact with other people who have different priorities and different time management skills. Some people will never be able to plan or manage their time properly, and their reasons are their own. They may not understand or agree with the way you choose to work, and their attitude and acceptance must be dealt with on a person-by-person level. A good deal of success in life is a result of the amount of interaction and networking that you employ to maintain visibility, approachability, and likability. It is not merely enough to be productive by yourself. You have to continue to "sell" yourself and advertise the comfort factor on a daily basis. This is the currency of credibility and acceptance.

Your people differ in their abilities and attributes. Some are morning people, others definitely aren't. Some are social and outgoing, and derive their energy from talking and interacting. Some are quiet and shy, some are leaders, while others are followers. Some love to structure their day and others prefer flying on a wing and a prayer.

This is very important to your Cool Time plan, since its concepts don't merely impact *your* day, they affect all the other people around you. How will they react to keystone time when up until now they were able to talk to you any time they wanted? If you start running fifty-five-minute meetings, are they the kind of people who can operate under tighter rules of discussion and interaction? The best recipe for success will come from a pragmatic combination of preparation, selling, and understanding the needs, motivations, and limitations of the people around you, with a goal of achieving 80 percent of your

Cool Time ambitions. Your community will most likely prevent you from achieving 100 percent—that's just how the world works, but excellence is always better than perfection.

YOUR BOSS IS A CONSTRAINT

I'm reminded of one Cool Time reader who later told me he had returned to his workplace and informed his boss that he wanted to reserve one hour each morning for keystone time. The boss dismissed his suggestion outright, saying that mid-morning was no time for sitting cross-legged on top of his desk, and that his yoga exercises would have to wait for his lunch hour. That's what he thought Cool Time was—he had no other frame of reference.

Most companies and their managers are looking for maximum productivity, minimum costs, and general advancement of their segment of the company, at least in the eyes of their own superiors. Change, especially when initiated from the field rather than from the traditional decision makers, can either be viewed suspiciously or welcomed warmly, depending on the outlook of the company's management. If we were to walk a mile in the shoes of our managers, we might discover that they are already working to a project plan, where the insertion of a new process may pose a threat.

It helps to remind the manager that Cool Time techniques always aim for personal and professional improvement. When applied correctly, they enhance productivity in practical, measurable ways. When *described* correctly, the Cool Time principles can sell themselves by speaking the language of win–win, such as:

- *Cool Time will improve the way in which I work.* Planned time management focuses on results through planning, communication, and implementation.
- *Cool Time will improve the way in which we work.* By allowing times for huddles, and by maintaining a visible, clear I-Beam Agenda, you and I can both understand what tasks lie ahead, and we can share in the responsibility of prioritizing them. This will reduce the surprises or miscommunications that can cause friction and cost time and money.

- *Communicating and communitizing:* By using branded concepts, such as keystone time and the fifty-five-minute meeting, I can share and explain the concepts and benefits of these techniques to my colleagues, which can lead to even greater productivity and clarity of communication.
- *Testing and measuring:* By maintaining an accurate I-Beam Agenda, we will be able to have more productive review sessions in place of the annual performance review.

Convincing a manager of the merits of Cool Time might be an exercise in selling. But think of the "hole in the house metaphor" used in Chapter 10 to describe the collective time wasted by small distractions. When you change perspective and focus on what motivates the customer (in this case your boss), on identifying his comfort concerns, on explaining how Cool Time would benefit him and his plans for the department he manages, you stand a greater chance of having Cool Time accepted and endorsed.

THE CALENDAR IS A CONSTRAINT

Every golfer knows that there is a small zone on the face of the club where the momentum and potential energy within the club head can be unleashed on the ball with maximum power. The same can be said of your kid's baseball bat. If you have her hold the bat with both hands, and you hold the other end firmly, you can then tap the bat in different places along its length. At one point on the bat she will feel no extraneous vibration from the hit. This is the sweet spot.

One of the key benefits of Cool Time comes from recognizing that the hours of the day, the days of the week, and the weeks of the year are not all equal in potential, and that a little higher-level thinking can go a long way in pinpointing the best times to do the right things the best way.

The day: As discussed earlier, the peak period of the morning is from 9:00A.M. to 9:30A.M., from which point our metabolisms spiral downward toward evening. The timing of meetings, keystone time, and other activities must be based on careful planning followed up by testing and measuring. Maybe morning meetings would be better, or perhaps a combination—morning meetings on some days, morning keystone times on other days. Your analysis will help to pinpoint the sweet spots of your day, which will have to be carefully guarded and used to their fullest.

The weeks and the months: Which weekdays do you think are more productive for you? Do you really think you have fifty-two Mondays, fifty-two Tuesdays, and so on at your disposal each year? In fact, just as our human metabolism is a wavering line of irregular energy, the same can be said about the working calendar.

And this doesn't apply only to you. If selling is part of your business, for example, which time of the week do you think is best for connecting with new prospects? Do you know? Have you tested and measured this? If you run meetings or conventions, when is the best time to guarantee maximum attendance? If you are a manager, or if you work for a manager, which days do you think would be best for coordinating projects or discussing goals?

Mondays, for example, are a time to get back into gear after the weekend. In many cases, people arrive back to work somewhat refreshed and ready to start again. Monday meetings have greater energy and the focus is on business and strategy. This may be great if you're chairing the meeting, but not so great if you're in sales, working the phones, looking to pick up new prospects.

Also, don't expect a level playing field on a Friday, the gateway to the weekend. By 2:00P.M., especially if the weather's nice, many people are already mentally out the door and on their way. OK, maybe this is not you, but this might describe many of your colleagues and clients. Some managers like to schedule meetings for 4:00P.M. on a Friday to ensure a punctual end. That's a little harsh (the fifty-five-minute meeting concept works much better), but it underlines the fact that no one likes to stay late on a Friday, nor should they have to. If you want to propose an innovative idea or make a great impression on a colleague or prospect on a Friday, you had better make sure that your pitch is truly outstanding because a lot of new ideas will be quickly forgotten if delivered on this day, especially in the afternoon. Same thing for calculating travel time. In many big cities the Friday rush hour starts early, say 2:00P.M. So getting across town to make one more client meeting on a Friday afternoon may be an exercise in frustration.

Public holidays: The seven-day weekend: A long weekend is a well-deserved rest that contributes greatly to our need for balance, but the problem with long weekends is that they're actually nine days long. It starts on the Monday prior. It's a little easier to get out of bed on a Monday morning knowing that a long weekend is coming up. People then experience a slow, week-long decline in productivity, mentally "checking out" by noon on Thursday as they begin anticipating the long weekend, which preoccupies their thoughts.

Can you imagine starting on a new project at 3:00P.M. on the Friday before a long weekend? Could you expect 100 percent commitment from your staff or colleagues? It's just not the best time to be starting things. Unfortunately, Friday comprises 20 percent of the available time in an average workweek. When people have their minds on the long weekend, their collective productivity potential is reduced. They may be there and be dedicated to the job, but the person they're trying to reach on the phone isn't there, or their mind is partially on the Saturday softball game, or on cleaning the garage, or on their long-weekend travel plans. The point is, due to the uniquely human ability to anticipate events in great detail, your people will be less than 100 percent tuned in between noon on Friday and noon on Tuesday, which adds up to two full days of work.

There are roughly ten official holidays in a North American business year, depending on where you live. So let's do some math:

- Ten long weekends equals ten Mondays or Fridays off. That's ten business days.
- The afternoon of the day before the long weekend, plus the morning of the day after the long weekend, are periods in which people are working to 50 percent capacity due to the change in mental focus. This is equivalent to five more business days lost (five Friday afternoons plus five Tuesday mornings).

This adds up to fifteen business days, the equivalent of three business weeks in which work can't get done.

Christmas and the holiday season: The annual Christmas season takes this notion of "lost work" and stretches it for weeks more.

People's minds generally start to drift away from work and toward holiday festivities by December 15, and do not fully recover until the first week of January. Face it. No matter how diligent and dedicated you might be, even if you personally don't celebrate Christmas, there are office parties being planned, lunch hours being stretched to allow for shopping and standing in lines, as actions and thoughts turn to this annual global event.

These festivities are well deserved, of course, and holidays of one sort or another have been held at this time of year for thousands of years. However, in terms of getting work done, it's essential to take into account the decline in productivity and attention that coincides with the holiday season.

The February blahs: Once the holidays are over, there are the February blahs. In North America at least, the diminished daylight, inclement weather, and a post-holiday anticlimax affects many people to varying degrees, resulting in lethargy, susceptibility to colds, and a general low ebb. Sometimes this escalates into chronic seasonal affective disorder (SAD). Again, this is a generalization, but even if you feel that you yourself are not affected by these blahs, it's entirely likely that a number of the people with whom you deal on a daily basis are.

Spring break: March ushers in the traditional spring break. Though this is a holiday for students, it's surprising (and gratifying) to see how many people turn it into a family holiday.

Summer holidays: During the summer months, people again start taking holidays, or at least have their minds on them, all of which is good for the soul and well deserved. However, from a project management point of view, having different members of your team disappearing at different times can be a daunting task and a real project constraint.

Halloween: Though it's not registered as an official holiday, October 31 is unique in the Western business calendar because it is a day when a disproportionately high number of people actually go home on time to accommodate a higher priority—spending Halloween night with the kids. Even for those without young children, the effects are noticeable—early traffic chaos and colleagues disappearing early in order to get home. My suggestion is to set a recurring alarm in your calendar for October 1, a reminder to review what you have scheduled for Halloween and assess whether it's realistic.

When you put it all together, you get this:

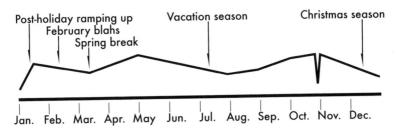

Figure 16.1: The trend line represents productivity, with the highest peaks in May and October–November representing the optimum combination of energy level, staff availability, and work focus. The sharp dip at the end of October represents Halloween.

COOL TIME DAY

The paragraphs above show just how few days in a year we actually have for true productivity. Remember, it's just a generalization intended to illustrate a point, but it's very difficult to see both the opportunities for best work and the traps that swallow up our time from a ground-level perspective. Since analogies and symbolism work so well to illustrate abstract points, I would like to invite you to observe a new event on your calendar: Cool Time Day.

Cool Time Day is based on a premise similar to Tax Freedom Day, which is the mythical date on a calendar when you have finally made enough money to pay your annual taxes, and everything else you earn until the end of the year goes to you.

Cool Time Day is intended to symbolize the true number of hours of productive work available to us within the course of a year. Its mandate is not to say "work harder," but instead to use this symbolic day as currency when introducing Cool Time techniques to the people in your world.

It works like this. (Remember, this is a generalization, but I think you'll find the pattern familiar.)

- Start with 365 days in a year   365
- Subtract 104 days for weekends $365 - 104 = 261$
- Subtract nine days for personal holidays
  and sick days $261 - 9 = 252$
- Subtract ten public holidays $252 - 10 = 242$
- Subtract the "weekend effect," the
  forty-two Mondays and forty-two Fridays per year
  in which 20 percent of productivity is lost
  because they are too close to the weekend
  $42 + 42 = 84$ days
  84 days × 20% = 17 days lost $242 - 17 = 225$
- Subtract the "long weekend effect," the
  ten afternoons before the long weekend
  and the ten mornings after the long weekend
  in which people are working to 50 percent capacity
  10 afternoons + 10 mornings = 10 business days
  10 days × 50% = 5 days lost $225 - 5 = 220$
- Subtract the "Christmas effect," the
  ten days before and after the Christmas holiday
  in which 20 percent of productivity is lost
  20 days × 20% = 4 days lost $220 - 4 = 216$
- Then if you accept that only 25 percent
  of the day is available for "real work,"
  the rest being set aside for meetings,
  phone calls, etc. $216 × 25\% = 54$
- Finally, factor in sleep deprivation,
  which increases over the course of
  the workweek. The decline in performance
  due to sleep debt, headaches, fatigue, etc.,
  means that people work to 75 percent of
  their true capacity. $54 × 75\% = 40$

Forty days of work per year. Is this reflective of your working environment? Take a moment to think about it. Your results might vary slightly, but all the components of this formula are common to the working environments of North America. More importantly, it underlines just how precious true productivity is, and how hard it is to see this when we're in the thick of it.

February 9 is the fortieth day of the year. According to these Cool Time calculations, this day represents the sum total of the productive time available to us within the year. All the other days up to the end of December are taken up with lost time, lost effort, and lost opportunity.

I propose that this day be recognized as a real event, like Labor Day. Call your colleagues together. Invite your boss as well. Have a donut, remind each other that spring is around the corner, and that real progress is being made, and can continue to be made. Cool Time Day does not stand for futility or frustration. Instead, it is an opportunity to review the concepts of "achievement" and "work" from a higher level, to reconnect with the plans and visions of the department, and most of all to communicate. It reinforces the value of intelligent use of time, including the adoption and practice of the concepts within these pages, such as keystone time, opportunity time, continual improvement, and, most vital of all, of working and living in Cool Time.

CHAPTER 17
COOL TIME IN THE HOME: THIS TIME IT'S PERSONAL

Home is the place where we should feel secure and unconstrained by the rules of the workplace, so is it really necessary to practice time management where we live as well as where we work? The answer is that whenever and wherever proactive habits improve life and reduce stress, they have a legitimate place.

THE POWER BREAKFAST

As we have already discussed, breakfast is an extremely important time. It provides an intake of nutrition after ten to twelve hours of fasting, and sets the stage for the expenditure of energy to come. A real breakfast is important, yet for many, it is sacrificed because there is "not enough time."

The nutritional importance of breakfast is discussed in Chapter 12, and finding time for a stress-free breakfast is discussed in Chapter 13. The bottom line, however—a point that bears repeating briefly—is that spending time in the morning to have breakfast in a relaxed manner while reading the newspaper or watching TV has greater value to your body and mind than the nine minutes of extra sleep that the snooze bar offers. Even if there are young children in the house who need help preparing for school, a quiet breakfast, perhaps enjoyed before they wake up, provides a stable platform upon which the stresses of the day can be dealt with and managed.

For those people who simply cannot do this—who simply cannot get up early for breakfast—there is another solution, and that is to have portable nutritious breakfasts available for quick takeaway. And this is best achieved through the use of Cool Time meal plans and shopping plans.

MEAL PLANS

By 4:00 p.m. on any given day, the majority of North American working people still do not know what they'll be making for dinner that evening. This presents a multilayered problem.

- *Mental energy wastage:* For a start, it means spending mental energy and attention at work trying to think of what to have for dinner. This may seem trivial, but given the small number of items that short-term memory can hold, it robs you of focus and productivity, which simply adds to your workload.
- *Disturbing your significant other:* Having to call your other half at work to engage a conversation along the lines of "What do you feel like for dinner tonight?" "I don't know, what do you feel like?" leads to even further distraction and stress. There are a million recipes available on the Internet, but few of them seem practical by late afternoon.
- *Time-consuming detours:* Once you finally decide on what to eat, inevitably there will be a need to stop off on your way home to pick up something, and this happens on personal time. Each little detour robs you of twenty to thirty minutes, which adds up to a great many hours over the course of a month. There are better things to do with this time, but it is time that is not perceived as "real" because, as we discussed in Chapter 3, it is uncontrolled and spontaneous.
- *Fast food as last resort:* So as four o'clock becomes five o'clock, the difficulty and frustration of deciding what to have for dinner increases, thanks to the efficient work of a hormone known as *ghrelin,* which is released into your system from your stomach, and which has little patience. It is not interested in rational thought. It just wants to be fed. The solution appears in bright yellow and red signage from every street corner: Fast food. But as we have seen,

fast food is not the best answer. Though major fast food companies have changed their menus in response to health-conscious customer tastes, the cooking oils, dressings, and other ingredients required to ensure a tasty and consistent product are no match for home-prepared meals.

Meal plans provide an excellent, time-sensible alternative to meals that come with a trademark after their names. One hour per week is all that's needed to plan seven dinners, lunches, and breakfasts, and to eliminate all the time wasters listed above. A week-long meal plan provides an opportunity for the family to enjoy balanced meals together. Time that would have been spent in stopping off at the store is now time that can be spent doing other things. Best of all, family favorites make meal planning easy. There will always be meals that can be repeated each week or so. Meal planning becomes very easy very quickly.

THE SHOPPING PLAN

For most people, grocery shopping is not the most interesting part of life. It is, however, a necessary activity and a time-consuming chore. But once you have created your week's meal plan (see above), the Cool Time approach to grocery shopping guarantees to cut the in-store time in half by creating a grocery list that prints items out in the order they are to be found on the store shelves. This means one circuit through the store. No doubling back, no wandering around. It may seem a little strange at first, but it is really nothing more than a project plan for the trip to the grocery store.[1]

The store map: First, map out the layout of the store on a piece of paper. Maybe you can do this during your next grocery shopping trip, or maybe you should make a special visit. (Remember the catapult analogy, page 184. Some things require investment before the dividends appear.) The map should identify all the specific zones of the store, including the aisles, the fresh fruit and vegetables section, the bakery, and the dairy section.

---

1 It requires little in the way of setup, and the templates and complete details are available at www.cool-time.com.

Next, envision how you might walk through the entire store, visiting each section only once, and give the sections corresponding numbers. For example, if fresh fruit and vegetables were in one corner, that might be section 1. Then above fresh fruit and vegetables is the bakery, which is section 2. Then there's aisle 1. The top of aisle 1, farthest from the cash, would be section 3, and the bottom of aisle 1 would be section 4. Then, if you were to turn your cart and head back up aisle 2, that would be section 5. The top of aisle 2 would be section 6, and as you turned to head back down aisle 3, that would be section 7. On it goes, up and down the aisles, until you reach the dairy, which is almost always placed at the back of the store. On your list, dairy might end up as section 20.

This looks like a lot of work, but the first time you observe your grocery shopping time shrink to one hour from two, you'll reap the benefits.

Now you have a map that will allow you to walk the entire floor area of the store in a logical, linear sequence. (This is essentially the same technique as e-mail, discussed in Chapter 10. It's about never having to do double work on mundane tasks.)

The next step is to work on your grocery list. Enter the items you typically purchase over the course of a week or a month into a Microsoft Excel spreadsheet. (The nice thing about using an Excel spreadsheet rather than paper is that you can add more items as you think of them, and sort them later.) Create four columns. (A sample Excel shopping list with hundreds of food items is available at the Cool Time website, at www.cool-time.com)

- Enter the word "Needed" as the first column header. This will be used later when you decide what to buy this week.
- The second column head is "Item."
- The third column head is "Sequence."

The number in the Sequence column next to each food item corresponds to the section on your store map where this item can be found. For example, avocado is a fruit, so it is located in section 1 on your map—Fruits and Vegetables. However, baking soda is located in section 8, at the bottom of the third aisle, near the checkouts. Yes, it takes a couple of trips to get this right, but the payoff is enormous.

When it comes time to do the actual shopping, review your weekly meal plan and enter how many of each item you need this week in the Needed column of the Excel spreadsheet. Next, read through the entire list in case there are other things needed for the household, the pantry, or the emergency kit. For items that are not needed this week, leave the corresponding cell in the Needed column empty.

When you're ready to print, choose Sort from the Data menu, and then sort by Sequence. Your shopping list will then sort in ascending order according to the numbers in the Sequence column. Why? Because this will give you a shopping list that presents your groceries in the order that you will encounter them as you walk from one side of the store to the other, up one aisle and down the next.

Finally, filter your list to show only the items that have a number in the "Needed" column. To do this, choose Filter and then AutoFilter from the Data menu. Then click on the downward-pointing arrow at the top of the "Needed" column, and choose Non-blanks. This will give you your list for the shopping trip, and will show only the items that you plan to buy this week. All the grocery items that you do not plan to buy will have no number in their "Needed" cell, and will be hidden during the filtering activity. The last thing to do is to print your list.

This is your Cool Time grocery list. You will now be able to move from one side of the store to the other, up one aisle and down the next with no time wasted. It will get easier each week as you update and refine this list, and the time you save can be spent on things more interesting than shopping for groceries.

And by the way, if you think this list is the product of someone who is just a little too obsessed with managing time, I can assure you that's not the case. In fact, it was devised as a solution for parents of infant children, a group that included me. Small children have even less enthusiasm for grocery shopping than adults do, but are more vocal at expressing their displeasure. Anything, therefore, that can help fit a week's shopping into the limited window of a child's patience is a stress reliever as well as a time saver.

CHECKLISTS

In Chapter 11 we discussed the importance of checklists as a tool for effective Cool behavior, since keeping track of the various items or activities that contribute to a successful project should not be entrusted to short-term memory.

Anywhere that checklists can be used around the house, they should be. Not only do they remind you of all of the items needed, they also allow for correct timings to be assigned, which increases the accuracy of preparation or travel times.

Every day, at train stations across North America, hundreds of people, a few dozen at a time, run across station parking lots desperately, hoping to make the train that is scheduled to depart in less than a minute. Where do they come from? Why do they do this to themselves, getting hot and stressed, risking injury and lateness? How did they misjudge the travel time to the station? Usually it's because of a casual and overly optimistic estimate of the time actually required to get to the station, based on a distance measurement taken one day when traffic was light and weather was good, when there were no accidents on the roads, and no ice to scrape off the windshield.

Cool Time travel checklists take such factors into consideration. How long should breakfast take? How long to get dressed? Do I have my important personal effects with me? How long will it take to get to the station tomorrow, based on this evening's weather forecast? As a family and as an individual, you can enjoy a healthier, safer life if you create and maintain checklists for:

- Getting to work on a good-weather day
- Getting to work on a bad-weather day
- Preparing the kids for school
- Packing for vacation
- Dealing with a power outage
- Dealing with an emergency such as coming home late (Who will feed the dog? Which neighbor can I call with a special request? Who will pick up the kids?)

- End-of-day checklists—take out the garbage, water the plants, lock the car, etc.

Checklists don't turn people into obsessive-compulsive list-keepers. Instead, they approach common tasks head on—tasks that will have to be dealt with anyway—and places them within a sequence and context that frees up more of the day for other life activities.

TIDYING

Given the short amount of time we have between getting home and going to bed, tidying can be as threatening as it is tedious. But we can use the principle called carryover momentum (Chapter 6) to help make tidying harmless. Carryover momentum states that one of the best ways of dealing with large tasks is to break them up into smaller, regularly scheduled activities, such as one hour a day, every day, at the same time of day, for a week or more. This not only gets things done cumulatively, it also tackles the procrastination problem of waiting for a single large block of time in the hopes of completing the entire task at once. To apply this principle to the chore of tidying, consider that, for those evenings when you're at home watching TV, small amounts of tidying can be easily factored into commercial breaks. Given that the average one-hour television show is actually fifty minutes long, that leaves ten minutes per hour available for tidying the kitchen and living room without cutting into your favorite show. It's simple and very effective. Every time your show goes to break, everyone does a little bit. The show comes back, and so do you. Over the course of one, two, or three shows, your living room and kitchen are returned to order, but not at the expense of your leisure time.

TWENTY MINUTES OF READING PER NIGHT

As a final Cool Time suggestion, remember to allow yourself twenty minutes a night to read something unrelated to work. Something you enjoy—not reports or memos or e-mail on your PDA, not something you feel you *should* be reading—something you really enjoy. Let those final twenty minutes before you turn out the light be a time to relax in a world far removed from the workaday world. This allows the body and mind to continue its work releasing the chemicals of high-quality sleep, setting the stage for continued excellence the following day.

CHAPTER 18
IN CONCLUSION: GETTING STARTED

THE NEW CAR SYNDROME

Once you decide to buy a new car, and you have the specific make and model picked out, a peculiar thing happens. As you go about your day-to-day travels, you'll notice that many people are driving the exact same car. They seem to be everywhere. It's not so much that there really are more of these types of car on the road than ever before, it's that you have set your mind to a new type of consciousness in which *you notice* this particular car more than you did before. Something in your mind has "switched on" and you have created the circumstances to recognize what was once just background noise. It's part of what is called reticular activation.

In the same vein, good habits beget other good habits by tuning your mind to them. When you undertake to tidy a messy room, for example, all you need to do is start with just one area. For a bedroom, make the bed. For a kitchen, clean just the sink area. This newly tidied zone will tune your vision and will help make another area of the room appear obvious as the next candidate for cleaning. Once that next area has been cleaned, another specific area will appear.

The same thing happens at work. As you develop proactive habits, your eyes and brain will perceive further opportunities, further improvement. Once keystone time has been established, it will make the processing of e-mail a candidate for improvement.

Once the idea of a 55-minute meeting has been accepted, drop-in visitations will be next to shape up. It becomes the beginning of a great and almost automatic procedure for continual success, and it's all inside you.

IS COOL TIME JUST A TREND? A FAD?

In considering whether to incorporate Cool Time principles into your own life, you may be asking why these techniques aren't already being employed in the workplace, and whether attempting to implement them would be dangerous.

I would suggest to you that there are two issues to consider here. One is that the diligent application of a technique such as Cool Time requires that you stick with the plan, review it regularly, and expend some effort in keeping on course, as we have just mentioned.

The other consistency is that of human nature to drift back toward a comfort zone of reduced effort and minimal complexity. Programs that are launched with great fanfare and promise tend to dissolve if not properly maintained. When faced with continued crises, pressures, and distractions, people find they just do not have the time to give to such maintenance. So the initiative fades, leaving only a memory and possibly a bias against trying it again. This is why the concept of the "pilot project" becomes so essential. Your colleagues need to have their needs for comfort-in-the-face-of-change addressed. They need to see where the project is going, and where the exits are. They need to understand what benefits they can expect and what threats might be lurking. The new techniques have to show their payoff before the "patience gate" closes.

GET STARTED

As with many great endeavors, the first step in integrating Cool Time habits may seem daunting and difficult as you face a challenge in modifying the momentum of your life and of the lives of those around you. Change requires dedication, but it must also be natural. There will be certain things that just will not go with your personality, your job, or your priorities, but everything must have a beginning. If you can resolve to follow a new plan of action, if you can commit to making the changes over a defined period of time without falling back, and if you review your actions and goals on a regular basis during that period, you will be able to fuel your actions, and the actions of your colleagues with the dedication and motivation needed for success.

Commit to a Cleanup phase. You may need a day or more to get started, to clean up your workspace, to file the files, and to "clean up" the current preconceptions of your workplace culture.

Tell yourself that this is the start of a new system, a system that will work, a system that will give you more time to do the things you truly want to do.

Factor in the changes pragmatically. Though you may wish to implement every single time management technique immediately, sometimes a wholesale change of office lifestyle may prove too difficult for you and your colleagues to take. Instead, set up a plan to factor in key time management techniques gradually, slowly influencing the timing of meetings, introducing the keystone time perhaps one day a week at the start, and "grandfathering" existing projects and priorities so as not to jeopardize current operations. Remember, your time management skills are designed to last a long time, and your success in implementing them may rely on easing them in gradually.

Use a buddy system. Consider starting out on the road to time management success with a colleague, perhaps someone with whom you work, or perhaps someone in a completely different business or office. Your mutual support and awareness will help maintain your time management principles and techniques, especially during times of weakness.

Schedule review periods. Regular reviews of your achievements and conflicts with the time management regime are crucial. Schedule a review period for one month, three months, six months, and a year after your kick-off date. Review your time management process regularly to refocus your energies and control the project itself.

THE CHANGE STATEMENT

Time management is about control—control over your own destiny, from the next few minutes to the rest of your life. It's a very personal system that requires diligence, tact, and communication skills in order for its several parts to interact neatly with the people, priorities, and activities of your world.

The techniques and principles mentioned in this book are suggestions that will need massaging and crafting to fit perfectly into your life. Many of them will help you, but they may take a little time to get right.

So in parting, I have an assignment for you while the Cool Time principles are still fresh in your mind.

1. Go to www.cool-time.com, and click on the "Change Statement" link, then print it out.
2. Write your most pressing time management problems on the Change Statement sheet, and, below, what you plan to do to change and improve these situations.
3. Then write down *why* you wish to change them. Identify and target the underlying motivation that will help keep you on the straight and narrow path to time management success, such as:

   - more time with your family
   - reduced stress at work
   - more control over meetings or projects
   - the ability to enjoy your Sunday without getting uptight over the approaching Monday

4. Note down also what you expect the resistance to be, and what tools/allies you have to help in successful implementation.

Then, if your resolve starts to falter, reread your statement. Reconnect with *why* these changes are important to you. Carry this document with you as your benchmark of success.

Of all the reasons for employing time management, I must confess the most satisfying of all for me is the knowledge that I have influence over my own destiny. Though there are always external issues to contend with, the control that I do have generates a satisfaction that fuels so many other motivations and makes every day so enjoyable.

Finally, please feel free to contact me at any time to ask questions, offer comments or suggestions, or to share your experiences in time management. The best way to reach me is via the "Contact Us" link at the Cool-Time website at www.cool-time.com.

Enjoy!

APPENDIX

COMMON OBJECTIONS TO
TIME MANAGEMENT

Nobody appreciates being told how to act. Books on time management often force people to adopt techniques that go against their
natural preferences, such as using a certain type of agenda, or doing
certain things at certain times—in short, taking some of the fun out
of life. Such fears and objections are perfectly sound, since people are
conservative by nature. Change generates fear of the unknown, a fear
of failure, or of being seen to fail. This fear goes back all the way to the
early days of our evolutionary history. Like the rest of our metabolism,
it cannot be changed so much as understood and properly channeled.

The purpose of Cool Time is to avoid strait-jacketing anyone by
allowing them and you to take the principles and apply them to your
environment, culture, and preferences in the most comfortable and
proactive way possible—the one with the greatest payoff.

Let's see if we can convince you and your colleagues by tackling
some of the most common objections head–on.

Time management doesn't allow for spontaneity. I'm the spontaneous
type. Time management *does* allow for spontaneity. In fact, it's perfect
for spontaneity, since it allows for the existence of "free time." By using a day plan to keep the day in order, spontaneous activities can occur without the risk that other activities and priorities of the day will
be endangered or forgotten. Taking some time for yourself is essential,

but in the real world this can work only if the other tasks are understood, prioritized, and accounted for.

It's good only for people in a routine, and that's not me. Everyone has a routine. Some routines are just more obvious than others. A person who does shift work, or someone who has a fixed list of tasks to accomplish day in and day out, has her routine clearly mapped out. However, we all have a routine by the very nature of the twenty-four-hour clock and our circadian rhythms. The first stage in effective time management is to step back, observe the constants and standards in your life, and then recognize the routine in which you operate. Then, like a fish suddenly discovering the water in which it lives, the patterns of your existence will emerge for you to manipulate and refine. If you can't identify any distinct routine on a daily basis, step back and observe your activities over a week or a month. Your routine will emerge, and will serve as the foundation for your time management plans.

It may work for others, but it simply won't work here. Our environment is too different. Everyone says that. Everyone thinks their business has unique pressures and requirements that make any time management regimen unworkable. Whether you work in the public or private sector, or a not-for-profit; whether you are a student, a homemaker, a manager, or an up-and-coming professional, you are in the business of selling "you" to other people. Also, no matter what activity you are involved in, there is someone somewhere who does it better, or did it better during her tenure. There is always opportunity for improvement, advancement, and refinement. It's up to you to identify how to make that happen.

I have no time to put together a plan. Actually, you do have the time; it's just been assigned to other tasks. Time is neither made nor found, simply rearranged, much like the law of conservation of energy we learned in Physics 101.[1] Let's put it this way. If you are a working parent, and your child's school calls to say that she is sick and needs to see

---

1 Julius Robert Mayer discovered the law of conservation of energy in 1842. It is now referred to as the first law of thermodynamics, and basically says that energy is neither created nor destroyed, just moved around. When combined with Albert Einstein's famous $E = MC^2$ formula, we get the law of conservation of mass–energy, which states that the total amount of mass and energy in the universe is constant.

a doctor, nothing would stop you from going to her side right away. Even if you're not a parent, a sudden toothache or a broken finger will change your schedule for the day pretty quickly. Most of your colleagues will be accommodating, and the work will get done later. The point is, time can be found when it's important enough. The benefits of Cool Time are tangible. They translate into money, health, satisfaction, and control. Cool Time is important enough to make the time.

I work better under pressure—I'm a last-minute kind of person. Nobody really works better under pressure, since pressure immobilizes higher brain functions and replaces them with the fight-or-flight reflex. In short, pressure instills mental paralysis. What last-minute people do well, as we saw in Chapter 15, is to compress their action and energy into a smaller block of time, not letting a project drag on, but keeping it on time.

When I need to, I just work harder—hard work equals more work. Hard work without planning is like working with an unsharpened blade. Huge amounts of energy go misspent, and sometimes it will not yield any product at all. You cannot make bread twice as fast by putting in twice as much yeast or by setting the oven twice as high.

I'm already organized, and I'm doing just fine. I have a system. I've used it for years. If you have a system that works for you and your colleagues in a satisfactory way, then that's great! Congratulations! Still, there is always opportunity for improvement. Take a moment to observe your current work environment and note whether certain tasks or procedures could be tightened up in order to save some more time. To be able to embrace change, it is necessary to confront your objections. Note any feelings of resistance you may feel toward continual improvement, and assess whether your arguments can be countered or whether your current way of doing things is adequate.

COOL *TIME* GLOSSARY

Answerholism: The irresistible urge to check new e-mail or voice mail, to the detriment of your true priorities. Based on a nervous system response to change.

Blue-sky: To stare up at the sky and to let your mind wander. A great way to regain clear thought and solve problems.

Carryover Momentum: The art of doing a task for one hour a day over numerous consecutive days, rather than over many hours in one single day. The mind is able to maintain creative momentum from day to day. This allows for large tasks to be broken up and dealt with effectively, and is a good tool against procrastination.

Circadian Rhythm: The daily natural rhythm that keeps living creatures in tune with the 24–hour day. Allows us to fall asleep at night and wake up in the morning.

Conditioning: Teaching people to act in a desired manner through positive reward.

Conditioned Reflex: A modern-day adaptation of an innate reflex, such as wanting to answer a ringing phone. The original "reflex" is in reaction to the ring of the phone. The conditioned reflex is the need to answer it.

Cool Time **Day**: The 40th day of the year, standing as a mythical symbol of our conceptions of busy-ness and productivity.

Critical Path: A Project Management technique that describes the shortest possible timeline for completion of a project, provided all goes well. Working to the Critical Path (such as a back-to-back, booked solid schedule) invites delay, overload, and stress.

Delegation: Empowering colleagues by educating them on the performance of a new task. Usually done in three phases. Delegation is not the dumping of a task onto another person, but an exercise in professional development and trust over time.

Distress: The correct term for what we usually refer to as "stress," a negative feeling of pressure and panic brought on by sensing a lack of control. The natural reaction is to revert to a "fight-or-flight" response (see below).

Emotional Bedrock: The confidence to know that *Cool Time* techniques are right, as they are based on sound principles such as Project Management, Physiology, and influence. Emotional Bedrock gives people courage when suggesting changes, saying "no" to additional tasks, and managing up.

Eustress: Positive stress, such as the rush felt by people who thrive on last minute situations or high-pressure jobs. So long as the mind feels in control of the situation, eustress can be a powerful productivity tool (for certain types of people).

Fifty-five Minute Meeting (also referred to as the 55-Minute Meeting): The technique of running successful meetings by making the end-time the primary incentive for prompt arrival and for active, focused participation.

Fight-or-Flight: A term that defines the natural reflex of most living creatures when placed in situations of danger or distress—to stand and fight or run away. Both, however, mean that rational clear thinking is replaced by instinctive reaction.

Huddles: Quick and frequent meetings with your manager (either scheduled or *ad hoc*) to ensure complete and ongoing communication regarding expectations and workflow.

I–Beam Agenda: The application of Project Management techniques (Planning, Control, and Closure) to each workday to ensure that a realistic project plan can be followed and that time can be properly defended.

I–Beam Review: The opening part of the I–Beam Agenda technique, in which the first 15 minutes of the workday are dedicated to realistic planning and prioritization.

I–Beam Base: The closing part of the I–Beam Agenda, in which the final 15 minutes of the workday are dedicated to closure (scheduling follow-ups, wrapping up loose ends), and improvement (*Kaizen*).

Kaizen: The principle of continuous improvement, in which you review your day and look for ways to improve your Time Management and work techniques on a daily basis.

Keystone Time: The most important part of your day—the period of undisturbed time in which you get your most important work done. It is essential to pair Keystone Time with Payback Time (see below).

Knowledge Base: A personal, searchable collection of facts, ideas and information, maintained and reviewed regularly.

Microcontent: Keeping e-mails and other electronic messaging short, relevant, and sent only to the right people.

Negative Value Time: When the time spent on work outside of work hours attains a value less than that offered by other activities, such as a being with the family or enjoying hobbies.

Opportunity Time: Extra time scheduled into each day to handle truly unexpected opportunities or crises. Parallels the concept of "lead time" factored into project plans by experienced project managers. Without Opportunity Time, workdays quickly revert to the Critical Path.

Pareto Principle: The 80/20 Rule. A concept that highlights how a majority of something good can be found in a minority of its context, as in "80 percent of a meeting's productivity comes from 20 percent of its duration," or "only 20 percent of all the material stored in your filing cabinets will ever be needed again."

Payback Time: Time reserved immediately following Keystone Time (see above) in which you "pay back" the people who respected your privacy during Keystone Time. Only by giving your people a guarantee of this suitable alternate can Keystone Time be truly respected and implemented.

Presenteeism: Being at work, yet being so tired or distracted as to not be able to function properly.

Project Management: The formalized approach to managing projects, by defining them as consisting of an identifiable task with a fixed timeline and budget and limited resources. The success factors of Project Management, as described in the Project Management Institute's *Body of Knowledge (PMBOK)* include planning, communication, and flexibility, as applied to a project's five phases: Initiation, Planning, Execution, Control, and Closure. *Cool Time* seeks to include Project Management concepts as the basis for successful day-to-day Time Management.

Reserved Activity: Scheduling certain activities as "recurring" into every day of the week, so as to reserve the time for them well in advance. *Cool Time* recommends that Keystone Time, the I–Beam Review, I–Beam Base, and lunch be scheduled as reserved activities.

Reticular Activation: The enhanced ability to notice or pay attention to certain stimuli, for example, after having decided upon buying a blue car, you suddenly become more aware how many other people have blue cars.

Schadenfreude: A German term basically meaning, "deriving pleasure in observing the misfortunes of others." My belief is that this is the basis for the huge popular interest in reality shows, which helps people balance their own sense of losing control of time.

Sensory Adaptation: Diminishing sensitivity to an unchanging stimulus, such as reminders posed on sticky notes around a computer screen.

Sixty-Second Qualifier: A short question or interruption that is allowed even during Keystone Time to ensure harmony in the workplace. Though interruptions are to be avoided during Keystone Time, if a colleague has a question that can be asked and answered in under a minute, it is best to allow for the question than to put it off to Payback Time.

SMARTS: A Project Management technique for identifying a project. SMARTS stands for: Specific, Measurable, Achievable, Realistic, Time-oriented, and Signed-off.

Stealth Messaging: Returning phonecalls after hours to take full advantage of voice mail, rather than getting trapped in small talk. Though this means bringing work home, it also allows people to get home earlier—an example of strength through flexibility.

Superhero Syndrome: The feeling that you can and must do everything, resulting in an inability to delegate, and an overloaded schedule.

Transition: The mental acceptance of change.

Triage: Battlefield prioritization technique for sorting out numerous casualties according to the severity of their injuries. If front-line emergency professionals can use effective rules for prioritization in high-stress situations, so can we.

Ultradian Rhythm: A natural rhythm that occurs *within* the 24-hour cycle. Examples include the 12-hour echo of the deep-sleep period of night, felt by many as the mid-afternoon doldrums, and the 90-minute cycle of energy and attentiveness that closely follows the patterns of digestion.

WIIFM: Stands for "What's in it for me?" and refers to the natural internal motivations of people to observe all activities in terms of their own need for comfort and security.

Workaholism: Addiction to the minutiae of work; performing work for work's sake.

REFERENCES

Arnot, Robert. The Biology of Success. Boston, New York: Little Brown & Co., January 2001.

Bing, Stanley. Throwing the Elephant: Zen and the Art of Managing Up. New York: HarperBusiness, 2003.

Bliss, Edwin. Getting Things Done: Timesaving Strategies That Make the Most of Your Day. New York: Career Track Publishing & Fred Pryor Seminars, March 1995.

Collins, Jim. Good to Great: Why Some Companies Make the Leap ... and Others Don't. New York: HarperCollins, 1991.

Greene, Robert, The 48 Laws of Power. New York: Penguin USA, 2000.

Hafner, Arthur W., Ph.D., M.B.A. Pareto's Principle: The 80-20 Rule. Seton Hall University, http://library.shu.edu/HafnerAW/awh-th-math-pareto.htm

Imai, Masaaki. Kaizen Institute, www.kaizeninstitute.com.

Lewis, James P. Mastering Project Management. New York: McGraw-Hill, 1998.

REFERENCES

Loehr, Jim, and Tony Schwartz. The Power of Full Engagement. New York: Free Press, 2003.Malanchuk, Maureen. Inforelief: Stay Afloat in the Infoflood. San Francisco: Jossey-Bass, December 1996.

Moine, Donald, Ph.D., and Ken Lloyd, Ph.D. Ultimate Selling Power. Franklin Lakes: Career Press.

Oncken, William, Jr. Managing Management Time: Who's Got the Monkey? Englewood Cliffs, New Jersey: Prentice Hall, December 1984.

Reardon, Kathleen Kelley, Ph.D. The Secret Handshake: Mastering the Politics of the Business Inner Circle. New York: Doubleday, 2002.

Robinson, Bryan E., Ph.D. Chained to the Desk: A Guidebook for Workaholics, Their Partners and Children, and the Clinicians Who Treat Them. New York: New York University Press, 1998.

Sun Tzu. The Art of War. Translated by Thomas Cleary. Boston: Shambhala Press, 1988.

Winston, Stephanie. The Organized Executive: The Classic Program for Productivity: New Ways to Manage Time, People, and the Digital Office. New York: Warner Books, February 2001.

INDEX

INDEX

INDEX

INDEX

INDEX

INDEX

INDEX

INDEX

INDEX

ending, 95, 99, 101–102

environment, 103–107

and ergonomics, 94

expectable task, *36*

fifty-five-minute, 63, 94–95, 179, 180, 207, 209

follow-up activities, 99, 100

on Fridays, 210

goals of, 94, 96

and I-Base Review, 49, 76

and implementation, 178

introductions at, 100

and lateness, 99–100, 169

minutes of, 99, 100, 102

on Mondays, 210

morning, 19, 75–76, 209–210

and new items, 101

and noise, 71–72, 105–106

number per day (stats), 93

officials, 98–99

on-time start of, 95, 99–100

optimum time for, 75–76

and Pareto principle, 94, 96

post-crisis, 89–90

predictable task, 31, 32, 33, *34*

refreshments at, 100, 106–107

reserved event, 37, *37*

running, 99–102

and selectivity, invitees, 102

small, two-person, 107

and timely arrival, 66, 168–169

upcoming, planning, 58

questioning need for, 93–94, 95–96

sample agenda, 97–98

venues, 105, 107

wrapping up, 101–102

(*See also* Toastmasters)

Melatonin, 18, 155

Memorization, 32–33 (*See also* Long-term memory; Short-term memory)

Mentors, 27, 196

Messages

email, outgoing, 132–133

leaving phone, 126–27

and setting up appointments, 127

stealth messaging, 128

voicemail, 122–123, 124, 126–127

Metabolism, 17, 18, *18*, 66, 151, 152–153, 160, 209, 231

Michelangelo, 53–54

Microsoft Outlook, 11, 37

Microsoft Word, 142, 143, 147, 148

Mini-meetings, 110

Minute-taker, 99, 100, 101

Mondays, 170, 210, 211, 214, 228

Monkey principle, 129

Morning

energy level, *18*, 19, 75, 83, 209

and I-Beam Review, 43, 44, *68*

routine, 169–173

Multitasking, 66, 85, 92

Murphy chair, 56

Muscles, 71, 147

Music, learning-focused, 72

Name(s)

call display, 125

contact list, backup, 140

filing system, 137

and voicemail, 123, 126, 127

ABOUT THE AUTHOR

 Steve Prentice is passionate about understanding how adults survive and thrive in the high-speed working world. In 1989 he graduated from Montreal's Concordia University with a degree in Communications Studies, and was also Valedictorian for that year. In 1990 he was nominated as a candidate for the Rhodes Scholarship while studying law at York University in Toronto. In 1991 Steve withdrew from the study of law, created his consulting company Bristall Morgan Inc., and has enjoyed great success as a speaker, facilitator, consultant, and media interview guest across the U.S. and Canada, teaching people about time, productivity, and career survival. In 2004, Steve returned to York University and is now working towards a Masters Degree in Psychology.